£1.25

WOODLAND WALKS
in Wales & the Marches

Webb & Bower
O︱S Ordnance Survey

WOODLAND WALKS
in Wales & the Marches
Gerald Wilkinson

First published in Great Britain in 1986 by
Webb & Bower (Publishers) Limited,
9 Colleton Crescent, Exeter, Devon EX2 4BY, and
Ordnance Survey,
Romsey Road, Maybush, Southampton So9 4 DH
in association with
Michael Joseph Limited,
27 Wright's Lane, London W8 5SL

Designed by Peter Wrigley

Production by Nick Facer

British Library Cataloguing in Publication Data

Wilkinson, Gerald
   The Ordnance Survey woodland walks in Wales
   & the Marches.
   1. Forests and forestry—Wales   2. Wales
   —Description and travel—1981- —Guide-books
   I. Title
   914.29′04858   DA735
   ISBN 0-86350-057-9

Typeset in Great Britain by Keyspools Limited, Golborne, Lancashire
Printed and bound in Great Britain by Hazell Watson and Viney Limited,
Member of the BPCC Group, Aylesbury, Bucks

TITLE PAGE
Native oak in Maentwrog wood: looking up.the
Vale of Ffestiniog into the heart of Snowdonia
National Park

Contents

Introduction

Over the years I have spent many weeks in Wales, North and South – not always looking for woods – but I cannot claim to know the country. Even knowing it, I am sure I should not quite understand it. Every Englishman must admit this.

How do you understand a landscape? Through its geology, geography and vegetation, no doubt, but more through some empathy with the people who have loved and exploited it, and modified its vegetation by use and cultivation. An introduction is perhaps no place for bits of autobiography, but I feel this is the only possible approach to the problem.

On my first visit to North Wales I learnt, on the easier slopes of Tryfan, that mountaineering was foreign to my nature. So be it; I could still admire the mountains, and with no danger of undue familiarity. What really impressed me then was the privy at the Williams cottage. It was a wooden bridge, with wooden walls and a suitable hole in the middle of a plank, built over a vigorous mountain stream. What could be more dignified or more sanitary? But what about Llyn Ogwen, downstream? . . . The water supply for the house came, of course, from further upstream. On a casual exploration of the stream I discovered the waterlogged corpse of a sheep.

Ever since these experiences I have failed to understand the Welsh character, and have failed to come to grips with the Welsh landscape, lovely though it is. On a later visit I walked through the clouds on the Miners' Track to find the romantic Castell y Gwynt – Castle of the Winds. In those days I carried a sketchbook, not a camera bag. The drawing was a complete failure, for I could cope with neither the mist nor the mystery of the rocks as they appeared and disappeared, as if travelling through steam. Coming down, I lost the track as well. It seemed in the end a waste of a day to spend it in the clouds chasing a rocky idea, but I suppose I was too impatient. I spent one very fine August Bank Holiday making hay below a Snowdon quite clear and divested of all

mystery. Hay in August – the first and only crop! The growing season is short here, just as in Pembrokeshire (Presceli) it is long, and produces potatoes in June. Such extremes are hard to reconcile in a little country: and there is a lesson in that. On another, rare, sunny morning I visited the Swallow Falls. There was no one about and I thought it was fairyland. But on my last visit to Snowdonia I dared not go near the place for fear of what thirty years of progress might have done to it.

I once stayed for a fortnight on Bardsey Island. It was meant to be a weekend, but we were marooned by the tidal race. Every day I sat in the sun on that hilltop out at sea, and watched the clouds build great pyramids over the Snowdon range. Fine weather in Snowdonia automatically makes rain, for in addition to catching the wet westerly winds, the mountains when warmed suck in the air from the sea, where it at once forms rain clouds as it rises: a nice Welsh paradox of the weather. This Bardsey holiday was another unique experience I failed to profit from. The island cows were dry and the fish tasted of diesel oil, but, worse than these, there is not a single tree on the whole island. My interest in trees had matured enough for this to cause real discomfort.

Of course, my whole approach has been wrong. I spent a week, once, exploring Anglesey in a vintage Delage that was too long for the corners and nearly too wide for the lanes, and obviously unsuited to the atmosphere away from Beaumaris. I have shared a sunny beach day after day with no one but the seals on the Pembroke coast, and have been many times to the Gower. But both Pembrokeshire – Presceli as it now mostly is – and Gower are curiously Englished, as if the real Welsh preferred their glistening mountain fastnesses. The same seems to be true of much of the Border country, including the Wye Valley: it is English as far as the hills.

Researching this book, I found myself crouching under a wall on the slopes of Cadair (formerly Cader) Idris, reflecting on the Welsh landscape. I know, but refuse to accept, that *cader* means a chair: to me it is a cratered cadaver. How symbolic is the natural excavation of this ancient piece of volcanic crust! Of course it is, as the geologist tells us, only a hard escarpment remaining from an infinitely ancient sheet of igneous rock that was folded to a peak somewhere in the sky above Trawsfynydd, then removed by some force unknown and unbelievable. The broken edges at Cadair and Snowdon were sculpted by the much more recent ice into their present shapes. Simple really, but it does not explain that dark mysteriousness.

Richard Wilson, the first of two landscape painters to have come out of Wales (the other was James Dickson Innes, who died very young in 1914), was born almost in the shadow of the Cadaver, early in the eighteenth century. But he went to Italy, then painted his mountain in a golden, classical mood. Turner, who looked to Wilson as a master, came here on a borrowed pony in 1798. He was only twenty-three, but his Welsh scenes, at least in his rain-spattered sketchbooks, are really true to life. In his paintings he aimed to include some literary themes, such as the extermination of the Welsh bards by Edward I. His picture of Dolbadarn Castle in the then very wild Llanberis Pass was his diploma work when he became the youngest RA in 1802: the picture still hangs in Burlington House. The gloom persists. Modern colour film does not respond well to grey skies; it sometimes catches the drama, rarely the mystery of the Welsh mountains.

An Englishman sitting under a wall below Cadair Idris, trying to understand the Welsh landscape, is surely a pathetic figure! Eventually it became dark and I strode down to the ragged tree-line and drove away, just in time to see a Landrover emptied of a load of rubbish. It turned down a no-through-road into the nearest village. The Welsh character had shown itself once again, and made a comment on the National Park.

In the southern valleys is the largest forest of Wales, Morgannwg, approaching 40,000 acres of spruce. Last year there were more than 750

fires and the Conservator described the position as embattled. But it was not the Forestry Commission that removed the native trees. Were the miners who scarred the valley sides, and then went deeper and built great slimy slag heaps – were they not Welsh? It was the Welsh, surely, who sold their water, and a great deal of land with it, to Liverpool and Birmingham, yet did not ensure local supplies. And it was the Welsh who built the main sewer out of Swansea much too short, so I am told. Which more or less takes me back to the Williams privy. Perhaps we should look at some figures.

Woodland, including all woods of over 5 acres of whatever species, in 1980 totalled 11.6 per cent of the land area of Wales, as against 7.3 for England and 12.6 for Scotland. The 1983 census of woodland by the Forestry Commission is a somewhat twiggy growth and rather technical, but I learn that Sitka spruce is now the most important tree anywhere in Britain; Scots pine the second. There is relatively little pine used in Wales. Wales has three times as much land under conifers as under broadleaves. The total is about 5750 acres, or $899\frac{1}{2}$ square miles of the total land area of 8016 square miles; so everyone in Wales, man, woman and child, has $4\frac{3}{4}$ acres of living space, of which $\frac{1}{2}$ an acre is woodland, much more than half of that being Sitka spruce. In addition there are eighteen or so good-sized trees, more or less isolated, for every person. These are not usually conifers, except perhaps in the fairly large category of 'clumps'. In England we have $2\frac{1}{4}$ trees per acre, but we have only $\frac{7}{10}$ of an acre of land per head, of which $\frac{1}{25}$ of an acre is woodland. These facts may explain why the Welsh have been a little careless with their native trees. Native woods are scarce now, but good examples are preserved by the Nature Conservancy Council and others. I have listed those I have not visited – some require permits and cannot be loosely described as walks. The ones I have seen have not been institutionalized and are not usually suffering from what would probably be called visitor erosion: in fact sheep-bite is a more serious problem, and fencing is needed.

The Welsh Forest formerly covered all the

land up to 2500 feet or more and extended beyond the present shores in several places – its remains are found in the sands of Cardigan Bay and Swansea. Small willows, the birches and the Scots pine were the first trees after the ice – which of course remained in the high cwms it had formed long after the lowland forest was established. It is said that the vegetation of Cwm Idwal on the side of Snowdon has remained unchanged since these arctic times, and many rare plants have survived on the rocks. Nevertheless, the peat of Cwm Idwal contains the pollen of deciduous trees. These trees lived in a period when the climate was warmer and at least as wet as our own. Following the final melting of the ice, pine became scarce; it is unknown in historic times in Wales. Willows and birch remained, retreating to poorer soils, and hazel spread rapidly. While Britain became islanded, the deciduous forest of Europe spread over the land. Alder, durmast oak and wych elm were the leading trees in upland Wales, while lime, ash, maple, beech and whitebeam thickly colonized the limestone and the lower river valleys, and probably much more of the land than could ever support them now, for the new soil was still 'base-rich'. The comparative height of most of Wales resulted in a more restricted range of trees than is found in England – with exceptions in the case of the whitebeams. It is not known how far the English oak penetrated because the fossil pollens cannot be separated.

That was the Welsh Forest, and only the mountain-tops were clear of trees. A cooler but still damp climate followed and reduced the forest. The soil began to be leached of its minerals while an iron pan formed below, limiting drainage. Heather and birch replaced much of the rich oak woodland. The forest was removed for ever as men and their animals began to alter the natural balance. Short-term agriculture made use of the forest as fodder, exhausted the soil of its humus, then left it to be grazed, so that trees could not return. Woods were retained for centuries in the valleys, but only while they remained useful, because there was always a shortage of richer pasture for fattening and wintering the beasts.

There was always enough wood, except in the mining valleys of the south. Timber was rarely used in building – even beams and posts were sometimes made of slates in unwieldy proportions. Then suddenly after the 1914–18 war there were whole valleys cleared of oaks, and these began to be replaced by conifer plantations, especially at first in North Wales. Soon, poorer moorland was being used for trees, deep ploughing being required to break-through the iron pan. Hill farms remained here and there as enclaves in the forest. Now the landscape has been completely redesigned, and Welsh voices are heard to say: that is enough.

Cyngor Gwarchod Natur, the Nature Conservancy Council, operates from three separate addresses in Wales:
Plas Penrhos, Ffordd, Penrhos, Bangor, Gwynedd LL57 2LQ for Gwynedd and Clwyd.
Plas Gogerddan, Aberystwyth, Dyfed SY23 3EB for Powys and Dyfed, except Llanelli.
44 The Parade, Roath, Cardiff CF2 3AB for Gwent, Glamorgan and Llanelli.

Nature Conservancy woodland reserves
Credydd Aber, near Bangor
Coed Gorswen and Coed Dolgarrog, Conway
Cwm Glas, Craftnant*
Coedydd Maentwrog
Coed Tremadoc, Portmadoc*
Coed y Rhygen, Lake Trawsfynydd*
Coed Ganwyd, Dolgellau (with NT)
Coed Rheidol, Devils Bridge, Aberystwyth*
Craig y Cilau, Llangattock, Crickhowell
Nant Irfon, Abergwesyn, Llanwrtyd Wells
Cwm Clydach, Brynmawr, Ebbw Vale
Oxwich, Gower

*permit needed

National Trust woodland nature reserves
Coed y Ganllwyd as above with Rhaiadr Du (Black Falls)
Coed Llyn Mair, Gwynedd,
South of Betws y Coed the Trust owns 25,820 acres of hills and valleys, mostly west of Ysbyty Ifan Village and around the high Llyn Conwy and the roads B4406 and B4407
Coed Llechwedd, Harlech
Lawrenny, Castle Reach, River Cleddau, South Pembrokeshire
Henrhyd Falls and Graigllech Woods, 11 miles north of Neath
Tintern: Wye Banks, 71 acres.

Key

The book is divided into sections which follow on numerically from west to east and south to north of the region. At the beginning of each section the relevant Ordnance Survey Landranger sheet numbers are listed. Each entry is headed with factual information in the form below:

       a   **b**   **c**

Burrator Forest *568 694*, ☿ ✸, *1000 acres, paths and a forest road, WA*

       d   **e**

a Ordnance Survey National Grid
   reference – usually of the nearest car park
b Type of woodland: ☿ deciduous
          ✸ coniferous ✿ marsh
c Size of wooded area
d Type of walk
e Owner of site

How to find a grid reference

The reference for Burrator Forest is *568 694*
56 – Can be found in the top and bottom margins of the relevant map sheet (identified at the start of each book section). It is the reference number for one of the grid lines running north/south on the map.
69 – Can be found in the left and right hand margins of the relevant map sheet. It is the reference number for one of the grid lines running east/west on the map.

These numbers locate the bottom left hand corner of the kilometre grid square in which the car park for Burrator Forest appears. The remaining figures of the reference (*568 694*) pinpoint the feature within the grid square to the nearest 100 metres as shown in the diagram below.

The following abbreviations are used:

AONB Area of outstanding natural beauty
CNT *County Naturalists' Trust*
CP Country Park
FC Forestry Commission
FNR Forest Nature Reserve
fp footpath
GLC Greater London Council
LA Local Authority
LNR Local Nature Reserve
MAFF Ministry of Agriculture Fisheries and
       Food
NC Nature Conservancy
NNR National Nature Reserve
NT National Trust
NTS National Trust for Scotland
pf private forestry
SSSI Site of Special Scientific Interest
SWT Scottish Wildlife Trust
WA Water Authority
WT Woodland Trust

Map of the Sections

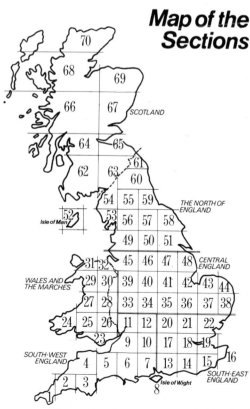

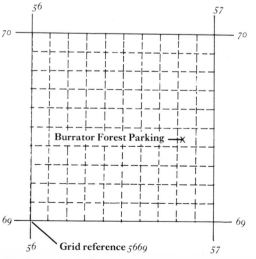

The dotted lines within the square

1:316,800 maps

RELIEF

Feet	Metres
3000	914
2000	610
1400	427
1000	305
600	183
200	61
0	0

274
Heights in feet above mean sea level

Contours at 200ft intervals

To convert feet to metres multiply by 0·3048

TOURIST INFORMATION

- Abbey, Cathedral, Priory
- Ancient monument
- Aquarium
- Camp site
- Caravan site
- Castle
- Cave
- Country park
- Craft centre
- Garden
- Golf course or links
- Historic house
- Information centre
- Motor racing
- Museum
- Nature or forest trail
- Nature reserve
- Other tourist feature
- Picnic site
- Preserved railway
- Racecourse
- Skiing
- Viewpoint
- Wildlife park
- Youth hostel
- Zoo

ROADS Not necessarily rights of way

- M 1 — Motorway with service area, service area (limited access) and junction with junction number
- M 62 — Motorway junction with limited interchange
- M 42 — Motorway under construction with proposed opening date where known
- A 1 (T) — Trunk road with service area
- A 15 Dual carriageway — Main road
- A 15 — Roundabout or multiple level junction
- B 676 — Secondary road
- Road under construction
- Toll — Toll; Road tunnel
- A 855, B 885 — Narrow road with passing places
- Other tarred road; Other minor road
- Gradient 1 in 7 and steeper
- 18, 23 — Distances in miles between markers

The representation on this map of a road is no evidence of the existence of a right of way

GENERAL FEATURES

- Buildings
- Wood
- Lighthouse (in use)
- Lighthouse (disused)
- Windmill
- Radio or TV mast
- Youth hostel
- Civil aerodrome — with Customs facilities / without Customs facilities
- Heliport
- Public telephone
- Motoring organisation telephone

ANTIQUITIES

- Native fortress
- Castle · Other antiquities
- Site of battle (with date)
- Roman road (course of)
- CANOVIUM · Roman antiquity
- Ancient Monuments and Historic Buildings in the care of the Secretaries of State for the Environment, for Scotland and for Wales and that are open to the public.

WATER FEATURES

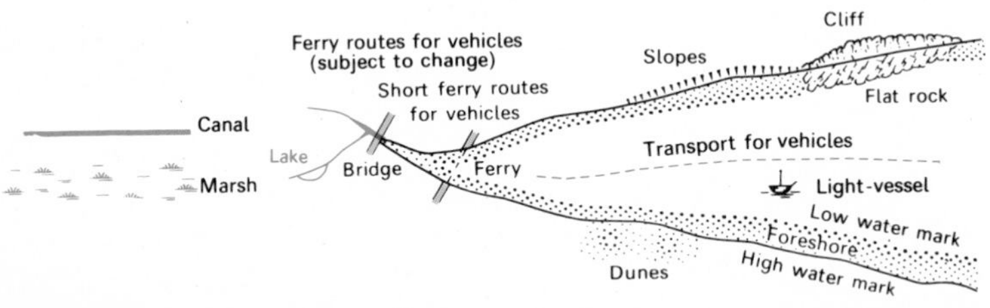

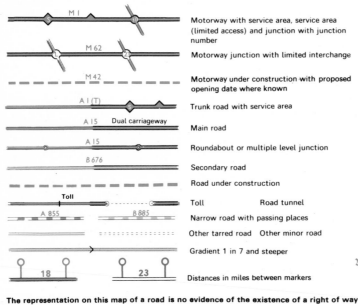

Canal
Marsh
Lake
Bridge
Ferry routes for vehicles (subject to change)
Short ferry routes for vehicles
Ferry
Slopes
Cliff
Flat rock
Transport for vehicles
Light-vessel
Low water mark
Foreshore
High water mark
Dunes

RAILWAYS

- Standard gauge track
- Narrow gauge track
- Tunnel
- Road crossing under or over
- Level crossing
- Station

BOUNDARIES

- National
- County, Region or Islands Area

1:50,000 maps

ROADS AND PATHS Not necessarily rights of way

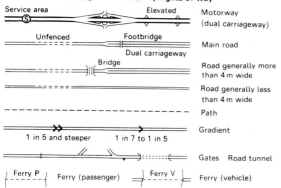

Service area | Elevated — Motorway (dual carriageway)

Unfenced | Footbridge — Main road

Dual carriageway

Bridge — Road generally more than 4 m wide

— Road generally less than 4 m wide

— Path

1 in 5 and steeper | 1 in 7 to 1 in 5 — Gradient

Gates | Road tunnel

 Ferry P — Ferry (passenger) | Ferry V — Ferry (vehicle)

PUBLIC RIGHTS OF WAY (Not applicable to Scotland)

- - - - - - - - - -

Public rights of way indicated by these symbols have been
derived from Definitive Maps as amended by later enactments
or instruments held by Ordnance Survey on and are shown subject
to the limitations imposed by the scale of mapping

**The representation on this map of any other road, track or
path is no evidence of the existence of a right of way**

TOURIST INFORMATION

i Information centre
P Parking
P
✕ Picnic site

✆ Telephone, public/motoring organisation
⌐ Golf course or links
PC Public convenience (in rural areas)
☀ Viewpoint

GENERAL FEATURES

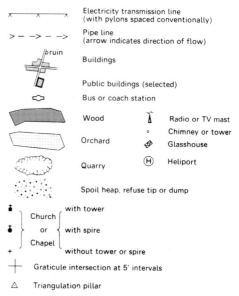

Electricity transmission line (with pylons spaced conventionally)

Pipe line (arrow indicates direction of flow)

ruin — Buildings

— Public buildings (selected)

— Bus or coach station

Wood

Orchard

Quarry

Spoil heap, refuse tip or dump

Church or Chapel
with tower
with spire
without tower or spire

Radio or TV mast
Chimney or tower
Glasshouse
Heliport

Graticule intersection at 5' intervals

△ Triangulation pillar

Windmill with or without sails   Windpump

HEIGHTS

·144   Heights are to the nearest metre above mean sea level

Heights shown close to a triangulation pillar refer to tne station
height at ground level and not necessarily to the summit.

WATER FEATURES

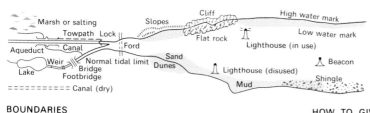

Marsh or salting
Towpath Lock
Aqueduct Canal Ford
Weir Normal tidal limit
Lake Bridge
Footbridge
Canal (dry)

Cliff High water mark
Slopes
Flat rock Low water mark
Lighthouse (in use)
Sand
Dunes
Lighthouse (disused) Beacon
Mud Shingle

ABBREVIATIONS

P   Post office
PH Public house
MS Milestone
MP Milepost
CH Clubhouse
PC Public convenience (in rural areas)
TH Town Hall, Guildhall or equivalent
CG Coastguard

BOUNDARIES

— · — · — National
— ○ — ○ — London Borough

— · · — County, Region or Islands Area
— · · · — District

ANTIQUITIES

VILLA Roman
Castle Non-Roman
⚔ Battlefield (with date)
☆ Tumulus
+ Position of antiquity which cannot be drawn to scale

The revision date of archaeological information varies over the sheet

RAILWAYS

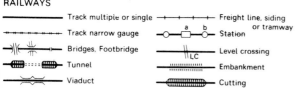

Track multiple or single
Track narrow gauge
Bridges, Footbridge
Tunnel
Viaduct

Freight line, siding or tramway
a b Station
Level crossing
LC
Embankment
Cutting

HOW TO GIVE A GRID REFERENCE (BRITISH NATIONAL GRID)

100 000 Metre GRID SQUARE IDENTIFICATION	TO GIVE A GRID REFERENCE TO NEAREST 100 METRES			
	SAMPLE POINT: The Talbots			
SN SO 200 SS ST 300	1. Read letters identifying 100 000 metre square in which the point lies.		ST	
	2. FIRST QUOTE EASTINGS Locate first VERTICAL grid line to LEFT of point and read LARGE figures labelling the line either in the top or bottom margin or on the line itself. Estimate tenths from grid line to point.		05	7
	3. AND THEN QUOTE NORTHINGS Locate first HORIZONTAL grid line BELOW point and read LARGE figures labelling the line either in the left or right margin or on the line itself. Estimate tenths from grid line to point.		70	7
IGNORE the SMALLER figures of any grid number: these are for finding the full coordinates. Use ONLY the LARGER figure of the grid number. EXAMPLE: 2**69**000m	SAMPLE REFERENCE		ST 057 707	
	For local referencing grid letters may be omitted.			

Common deciduous trees in Britain

field maple
native on chalk
and limestone
in woodland
and hedges

Norway maple
planted, usually
for decoration,
sometimes
naturalized

sycamore
introduced from
S. Europe before
1600. Fine timber
but now a weed

wild service
native *Sorbus* of
ancient woods.
Brown berries –
'chequers'

London plane
hybrid, street tree
timber is
'lacewood'

Guelder rose
native shrub
of damp woods
and hedges

white poplar
young leaves
5-lobed, all are
white beneath.
'Abele' tree

sessile oak
acorns without
stalks. Native
and rarely
planted

pedunculate oak
acorns on stalks.
Native English
oak, often
planted for timber

Turkey oak
long planted,
naturalized in S.
Red oak (right)
amenity tree from
N. America

Swedish whitebeam
imported hybrid
Sorbus, true to
seed, a neat tree
for parks, roads

hawthorn
hedge, left, and
woodland or
Midland, right:
May blossom

whitebeam
commonest native
whitebeam, *Sorbus
aria*. All love
limy soils

Wych elm
native to
all Britain

English elm
or field elm, tall,
now almost extinct
but sucker shoots
still grow

**Smooth-leaved
elm** one of several
natives such as
Cornish elm,
Plot's elm

hazel
common small tree
of hedges and
oakwoods, often
coppiced

hornbeam
native to S.E.
woods, once
valuable as
firewood

beech
tallest native of
best-loved woods,
also used in
shelter-belts

cherries
bird cherry and gean
or wild cherry,
plums, crab apple
and sloe

alder buckthorn
now uncommon
native of damp
woods in the
south

buckthorn
native shrub.
Flowers (green)
& berries stalked
from axils

dogwood
native reddish
shrub. Flowers
(white) & berries
in round clusters

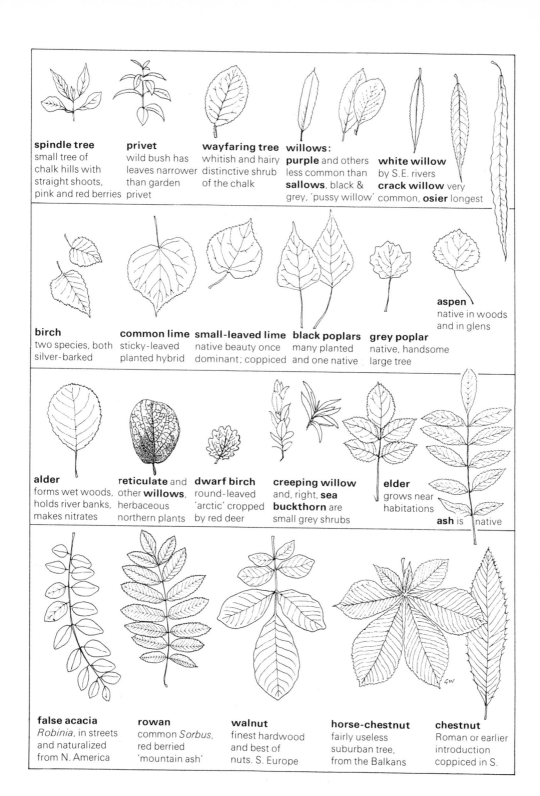

spindle tree
small tree of
chalk hills with
straight shoots,
pink and red berries

privet
wild bush has
leaves narrower
than garden
privet

wayfaring tree
whitish and hairy
distinctive shrub
of the chalk

willows:
purple and others
less common than
sallows, black &
grey, 'pussy willow'

white willow
by S.E. rivers
crack willow very
common, **osier** longest

birch
two species, both
silver-barked

common lime
sticky-leaved
planted hybrid

small-leaved lime
native beauty once
dominant; coppiced

black poplars
many planted
and one native

grey poplar
native, handsome
large tree

aspen
native in woods
and in glens

alder
forms wet woods,
holds river banks,
makes nitrates

reticulate and
other **willows**,
herbaceous
northern plants

dwarf birch
round-leaved
'arctic' cropped
by red deer

creeping willow
and, right, **sea**
buckthorn are
small grey shrubs

elder
grows near
habitations

ash is native

false acacia
Robinia, in streets
and naturalized
from N. America

rowan
common *Sorbus*,
red berried
'mountain ash'

walnut
finest hardwood
and best of
nuts. S. Europe

horse-chestnut
fairly useless
suburban tree,
from the Balkans

chestnut
Roman or earlier
introduction
coppiced in S.

13

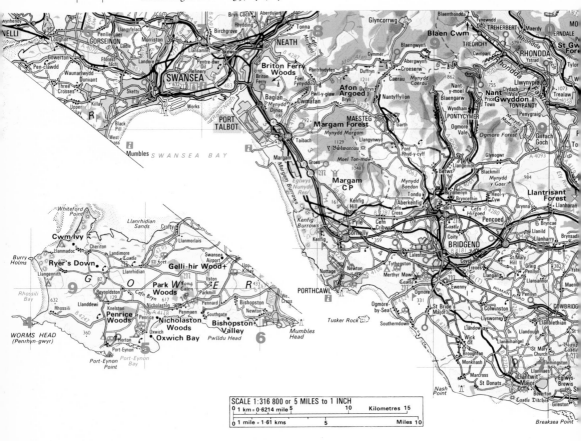

SCALE 1:316 800 or 5 MILES to 1 INCH

For English visitors two main routes westwards tend to iron out the north-south intricacies of this region, suspected to contain little but chimneys, chapels and choirs. From the upland route, the Head of the Valleys Road, the A465(T), a descent into any one of the valleys will reveal surprising riches, both municipal and arboreal. The road itself reveals moorland and occasional stunning hillsides of colour-patterned, tiny houses and gigantic, purple pit tips, already assimilated into the landscape. On the southern route the excitement of the Severn Bridge is soon forgotten on the motorway, which looks like any other except for the oddity of bilingual

signs. The wide pastoral Vale of Glamorgan is ignored, and, looking forward to Gower or Pembrokeshire, we rarely have time to stop. I tried turning off at junction 27 for Ebbw Vale.

Ebbw Forest: *Abercarn village 216 945, Forest Drive,* **Cwmcarn** *220 932,* ♣*, various walks and picnic places, FC*
The forest drive is clearly signed from the valley road, the A467, but the entrance was locked in October. This is a 7-mile drive with promising picnic places and walks en route. Thus disappointed, I followed the Forestry Commission instructions for Nant Gwyddon picnic place and got lost on a built-up hillside.

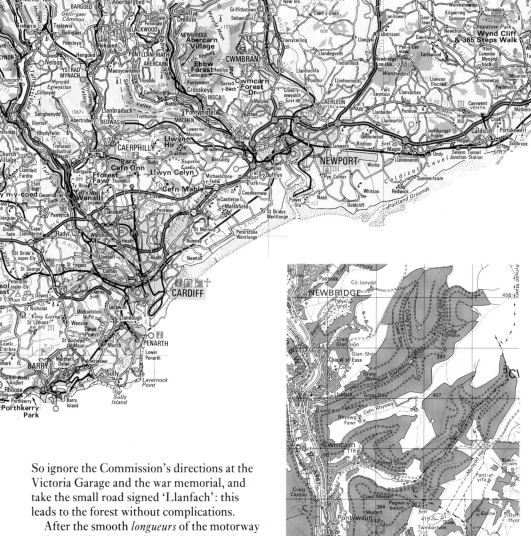

So ignore the Commission's directions at the Victoria Garage and the war memorial, and take the small road signed 'Llanfach': this leads to the forest without complications.

After the smooth *longueurs* of the motorway and the ordinariness of the industrial valley, the terrific height and steepness of the forest is exhilarating and even heavy rain could not obscure the grandeur of the landscape. Take the right fork, not signed, for the picnic place, where no doubt the Forestry Commission will have repaired the effects of a recent fire. The foresters here deal severely with native trees that dare to intrude. They have worse menaces to worry about.

NEAR CARDIFF

Other Ebbw Forest picnic places, with walks, are at **Llwyn Celyn**, *202 855*, **Llwyn Hir**, *206 866*, and **Cefn Mably**, *209 843*, all approached from Lisvane, north of Cardiff. Here also is **Parc Cefn onn**, 158 acres, with a wooded valley planted with rhododendron, azalea,

Forestry above Treherbert, Rhondda

bamboo, cypress, *Pieris*, *Berberis*, willow and water-lilies. There is a railway station in the middle and older woodland to the north with large specimen trees around an artificial pool.

In the village of St Fagans, 4 miles west of Cardiff centre, the 'Castle' and grounds contain the Welsh National Folk Museum with resident craftsmen producing traditional wooden ware, basketware, etc, and some reconstructed buildings with fascinating details in oak and wych elm. Hazel hedges are laid in exemplary style and there are fine planted beeches, and a generally bosky atmosphere in the grounds. To the south, just west of Barry, is **Porthkerry** Country Park, *099 673*, with mature woodland of native trees on the limestone cliff top. Nearer to Caerphilly is the new Forestry Commission plantation of Coed Coesau Whips, with walks from *202 854*, the car park, and one from the forest entrance, *200 866*, near Rudry village.

Two miles east of Cowbridge is the Forestry Commission's Tair Onen Nursery, with an average 25 million seedlings in stock, and in the **Hensol Forest** north of this, two picnic places with walks, *038 764* and *033 768*. These are easily reached by turning south from junction 34 of the motorway. North of the M4, beyond Llantrisant, is a picnic place, *025 845*, among larches dating from 1922. **Llantrisant Forest** is one of the earliest Forestry Commission plantations. Turn north from the A473 (Llantrisant to Bridgend) after Talbot Green, at the humped-back river bridge. Still north of the M4 is Tŷn-y-coed picnic place at *084 826* – a young plantation with old native trees retained.

Very near to the city (and junction 30 of the motorway) the village of Tongwynlais and the nineteenth-century folly of Castell Coch are on route for the **Fforest Fawr** picnic place, *143 838*, in deciduous woodland with many

Ebbw Forest near Abercarn

pathways. **Wenallt**, *153 832*, a mile south-east, has nature trails run by Cardiff city, 140 acres of woodland and heath.

Cardiff city has worked hard to preserve and provide access to surrounding woodlands and has produced two excellent series of booklets: *Nature Trails*; *Wenallt, Bute Park, Cefn-on, Coed Coesau Whips, Glamorgan Canal and Caerphilly Common* and the *Take a Walk in the Parks* series, including Cefn-onn Walk, Nant Fawr, Llandaff, Taff Valley. These overlap at several points as can be gathered. Bute Park for instance is in the Taff Valley, and also happens to be 200 yards from City Hall – the trail begins grandly with a *Ginkgo* and a *Paulownia*. The booklets are not afraid to be obvious, but usually contain something new, and are illustrated in a bold and original style by Uwe Santore, who expresses a sense of discovery, even when drawing a bluebell. The authors clearly understand that one can take nothing for granted.

MARGAM, RHONDDA AND CYMER FORESTS

The forests of Neath and Glamorgan – Coed Ffranc – were, in historic times, great producers of oak fuel, while coal quite near the surface waited for the nineteenth-century canals and railways. The coppices were then used for pit props, first in drift mines, driven into the hillsides. Deep mines followed, adding their waste-tips to the scars of the 'levels'. Coal was exported to France and pine timber from the Landes came to Wales as pit wood. When in the 1930s many thousands of miners were out of work, reafforestation of the hillsides, and even of the slag heaps, began, with large forests of spruce and pine planted by the Forestry Commission. Now the Commission's Coed Morgannwg (which includes Margam and Cymer), with Rhondda, covers about 40,000 acres of forest land.

Rhondda
North of Pontypridd are picnic places at *033 957* and *046 966* in the St Gwynno Forest. **Nant Gwyddon**, *987 945*, north of Tonypandy, has a walk of $1\frac{1}{2}$ miles.

In the Rhondda, with **Treherbert** as the centre, are three forest walks. Blaencwm to the summit of Pen-pych is steep – park by the disused railway bridge, *923 990*. Two others start from points on the A4061 north of Treherbert.

Margam Country Park, *814 851*, embraces eight centuries of privileged land-use from Cistercian abbey to nineteenth-century Tudor-Gothic castle. It is now patrolled by a battered single-decker bus, which carries park-and-ride visitors to the finest orangery in the world (a very fine building restored to contain both orange trees and public gatherings), stopping at the nicely converted centre and café. Modern sculpture was added all over the landscaped deer park in 1983, not to my mind with great success but certainly adding interest. Trees are mainly Scots pine in various shapes and sizes; very sculptural anyway in the open. Specimen conifers and broadleaves, above rhododendron, are between the castle and orangery. A slide-and-sound show in the excellent small theatre dwells rather too fondly

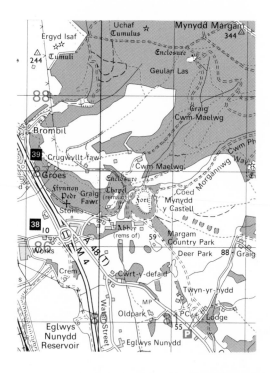

Natural sculpture in Margam Country Park

on the annual deer cull. However, this is not an event that visitors can take part in.

There is a long walk to Afan Argoed, part of the 23 miles of the Coed Morgannwg Way.

Afan Argoed *821 951*, ♀ ♣, *7 forest walks, ½–5m, CP, (CC and FC)*
All the walks including the Michaelston Forest walk of 5 miles, and the Argoed walk (leaflet guide) in remnant oak woodland, 2 miles, start from the centre, which has a Miners' Museum and other exhibits, and a snack bar open in summer. There is a separate Rural Studies Centre with a resident teacher. The five easier walks are all mapped in a single leaflet issued by West Glamorgan County Council, and all explore the 140 acres of the Country Park within the enormously larger context of the forested hills and high moorland.

An Afan Valley scenic drive leads to the Rhondda and there are Forestry Commission picnic places as well.

In the Ogwr Valley at Allt y Rhiw are 120 acres of original sessile oak coppice.

There are walks with views of the sea on the oak-covered cliff above **Briton Ferry**, near Neath, *745 940*. The Neath Canal at Tonna is beautifully wooded.

GOWER

With all its forests and country parks, South Wales still presses heavily on its little 14-mile

appendix for the elements of natural countryside. In summer the pressure seems almost too great as an endless procession of cars and caravans winds its way to the Gower beaches, but inland countryside remains undisturbed. The peninsula is unspoilt, which is to say that industry stops at its neck. Suburbia begins, but is miraculously checked at the cattle grid near the airport. The whole peninsula is an Area of Outstanding Natural Beauty and the National Trust has no less than 16 properties, totalling 4675 acres. Much of this has had to be fought for: Nott Hill, *528 887*, for instance, 5 acres of rock and bracken near Penmaen, was bought as several building plots, lot by lot, by a Miss Lee in 1955.

The theme of Gower is moorland and coastland, the latter intricate on the south and desolately marshy on the north. There is no primary woodland, except perhaps at Gelli-hir, but limestone cliffs and valleys are rich in vegetation.

Oxwich Bay *502 865*, ♀, *3m including cliff-top path, NNR*
The woodland walk starts at the church on the cliffside, to your right as you enter the beach car park. Most of the beach, over a mile wide, as well as the dunes and the marshes (for which a permit is required) are part of the nature reserve, and the beach is very crowded in summer. The Nature Conservancy has a busy centre here.

Stick to the footpaths: with several thousand visitors here annually the wood could soon become degraded. Sycamore is also a threat, and has to be cleared. There are old field boundaries within the wood, as well as limestone quarries. The path emerges onto bracken, gorse and grassland, returning via the cliffs and then through an old hazel coppice to Oxwich village.

Nicholaston Woods, on the north side of the bay and inland from the Burrows, which are a National Trust property, also have a footpath which emerges onto the road out of the bay at *503 882*. There is a little parking space here if you are early or late, before or after the crowds. There is also a footpath 'To Nicholaston Woods' signalled on the road one mile west of Penmaen. This is recommendable, not so much for the rather dreary secondary woodland – but you may be grateful for the shade – as for the exit onto the dunes. The beach is wide and lightly strewn with rusting cans, but the sight of blue butterflies on gorgeous blue sea holly is worth the walk – 2 miles, about.

Penrice Woods: Millwood *488 883*, ♀ ⚲, *350 acres, walks ¾m and 2m, FC*

Turn off the main road, the A4118, opposite a prominent converted granary on stilts, down a steep and narrow tunnel of a lane which ought to lead to a wonderland. The Commission's Coed Abertawe (Swansea Forest) is not that, but the trees here are tall and vegetation generally at least lush where a picnic place has

been made by the reconstructed mill pond. The longer walk through young spruces and beeches is dull, but it's a walk.

Also on the south coast is the National Trust's **Bishopston Valley**, 153 acres, from Kittle, *574 894*, to quiet Pwlldu Bay, with 'hanging woods'. The coastal scenery is more impressive than the woods, and a beach that can't be reached by car is a great rarity.

Park Woods, Parkmill *547 892*, ♀ ⚲, *3m of roadways, FC*

The map reference, as usual in this book, is for the car park, here on the far side of the busy shop at Parkmill. There really is nowhere else to park. Green Cwm is the official name of the valley, technically a dry limestone one, which extends and divides north and west from the pretty ford at the north-west corner of Parkmill village. Magnificent larches seem to reach the sky from the deep cwm over a mixture of native trees with much holly.

A footpath from Gower Inn, Parkmill, to Ilston church is through private woodlands in Ilston Cwm.

Gelli-hir Wood *562 925*, ♀, *71 acres, fp, NNR*

Turn off the B4271 at Fairwood Common for Cilonnen. *Gelli-hir* means long grove: the wood is narrow. Wet oak-birch woodland with alder leads to ash and wych elm with small-leaved lime: there are interesting pools; but most impressive was the sudden immersion in true ancient woodland. In the grass were yellow pimpernel and cow wheat. A former warden, the only other soul encountered, spoke of neglect, but I liked it like that.

Cwm Ivy *439 937*, ♀ ⚲, *dunes, fps, NR*

Turn right at Llanmadoc church. Parking is not now available at the farm of Cwm Ivy, which has recently lost its remarkable owner

LEFT: tall beech, Penrice Woods. The beech is in the castle grounds where a footpath leads to Oxwich or inland into the woods.

OPPOSITE ABOVE: Hills Tor, Whiteford Burrows, with Corsican pine and Welsh Blacks

BELOW: Whiteford Wood, Monterey pines

Woodland spreads with sallows and thorns to the pasture of Ryer's Down

and her tame goats. The path straight on leads down to the dunes of Whiteford Sands over dreamy slacks where hawthorn, burnet rose and dewberry are populated by thousands of grasshoppers. Above on the grey Hills Tor, Welsh Blacks cling like flies. A delicate wood of Corsican pines lightly anchors the sands, and the pines are spreading, self sown, in places. Slightly inland is an avenue of sturdy *Pinus radiata*, Monterey pine – past the warden's

house. This is a good short walk on a wet day. You can continue to the open marsh, where marshmallows bloom in a shade of mauve which would be vulgar anywhere else, and return alongside Cwm Ivy Wood, a collection of noble ashes rising above larch and beech plantations.

On **Ryer's Down**, *451 920*, part National Trust and very lightly grazed by two or three of the Gower's semi-feral ponies, sallows, blackthorn and ash begin to invade from the background of a sycamore wood. A new woodland walk is almost there; a good place for a picnic. Do not feed the ponies: they bite.

West Wales

There are Forestry Commission sites near Blackpool Mill (a working mixed wood near the Eastern Cleddau), *064 145*, 4 miles west of Narberth. Blackpool Mill is an agricultural museum. The car park is at a viewpoint for the Pembrokeshire National Park. A waymarked walk of a mile or so can be extended to 5 miles.

In the Gwaun Valley, east of Fishguard, are two sites at *006 348* and *045 349*, with another picnic place at Pontfaen, in between. Near **Cenarth** are two woodlands: one has a Forestry Commission walk and picnic spot, *264 406*; nothing memorable except for the cleared and planted part of the wood (through the white gate) which has strangely retained the sense of a woodland place, though of course the spruce and larch will eventually suppress this. The indicated walk is a polite one, among broadleaved trees, in a tiny stream valley fenced for safety. The other wood, Tyddyn du, on the opposite side of Cenarth is even less prepossessing.

Coed Tyddyn du *272 426*, ♀, *47 acres, SSSI, WT*

'Farming was abandoned here at the end of the nineteenth century and the woodland has been allowed to develop entirely without man's interference.' (Woodland Trust Leaflet) Following the directions, I entered the wood at the map reference. A good path leads through trees to a field in which there were a caravan with a pile of old tins, and a genuine-looking North American Indian lodge, teepee or wigwam. No one seemed to be about, though a bicycle leant on a tree. The wood all around is extremely overgrown and progress through would only be possible using an axe or billhook, SSSI or no. Parking by the (occupied) remains of the farm is awkward. At present this cannot be a recommended woodland walk.

Pencelly Forest *134 396*, ♀ (♠), *162 acres, fps, NNR (and FC)*

This is almost certainly the most beautiful wood in Wales. Although I had a brief flash of sunlight, as can be seen from the picture on page 24, towards evening, my visit was in extremely stormy conditions and I did not see much of the lower part of the wood. Even so, the coppiced oak of the upper, drier part is close to perfection and of the greatest interest, well justifying a long journey to see it. There

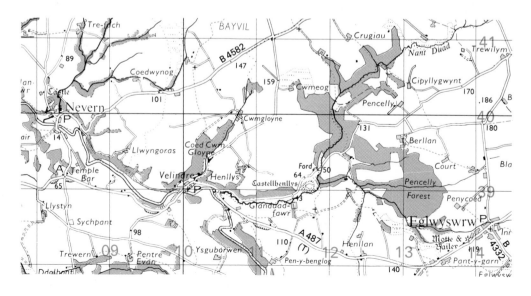

are some hazel and beech; ash and alder are dominant on lower ground. The wood is now sheltered from the west by Forestry Commission larches, a belt of which is apparently to be left standing although clear felling is in progress. Bits of woodland by the lane are also richly beautiful.

is not wooded. It should be said, though, that valleys below the level of the plateau, and even walls, are extremely richly endowed with plant life. All scraps of woodland are of interest here. While the rest of Wales is forested to the point of stupefaction, Pembroke remains dearest to the heart of the naturalist. The people also are

Beech tree in Pencelly Forest

The 'Forest' occupies a double valley north-west of Eglwyswrw on the A487(T) between Cardigan and Fishguard. The more romantic of two entrances forks from the main road $\frac{1}{5}$ mile east of Velindre (*after* the road to Moylgrove). There are several grassy, shaded lay-bys on this little road, which continues over a ford and nearly 2 miles to the oakwood, which is clearly marked as a nature reserve. The ford will be too deep for most cars after heavy rain. There is a footbridge. To enter from Eglwyswrw turn off the main road opposite the inn, go past the garage and left, right and left along the farm lanes. There is a space to park just inside the shelter of the larches; or perhaps you will avoid storm-force winds! The *Nature Reserves Handbook* mentions *Crataegus laevigata* and aspen, both very localized in West Wales. One hundred and twenty species of flowering plants and ferns are recorded, we are told.

The Pembrokeshire National Park is of course largely coastal (and includes the greater part of this coast), and the plateau or peneplain

Coppice oaks, *Quercus petraea*, Pencelly Forest

Patterns of forestry in Pencelly Forest

Sinister hills of Pembrey

friendly and kind.

Coed Abertawe flourishes also, north-west of the city where the M4 sweeps over a series of forgotten valleys before turning north to Cross Hands and Tumble on its way to Carmarthen. Hiding below junction 47 is a deeply shaded parking place and the disabled trail of **Afon Llan**. Choose a fine day, for it can be slightly depressing down here in the rain. I didn't attempt any of the other walks.

Pembrey *402 005,* ⚓ *, 519 acres, several trails, easy walking generally, CP*
Only a comparatively small part of the Pembrey Forest forms the seemingly endless dunescape of the Country Park. There is a Forestry Commission picnic place and a walk in the pines close to the housing estate of Pembrey, and you get an idea, as you cross the railway bridge, of what happens to old caravans when they die. But the road to the Country Park takes you smoothly to the many acres of parking space which are sheltered below the shoreline dunes. The shore is

untouched by the hand of man, except for the planting of marram grass – actually sprayed on along with a coat of fixative. The openness and freedom of the place, its little dry hills and nicely grouped Corsican pines and sea buckthorn, make you want to walk – and you can walk anywhere at any time; but there is a portentous undertone.

You soon notice that most of the hills have flat tops, straight sides and holes through the middle. They are old loading bays for high explosives, which were manufactured here for 80 years. If the idea of making bombs does not quite fit in with your idea of nature walks, then I can only sympathize. The RAF drives the point home with noisy mock dogfights over Carmarthen Bay. Across the shallow sea the Gower lies grey, bordered by the more innocent dunes of Whiteford Burrows: but it is a longish drive round. Perhaps we shouldn't be so squeamish, but I wonder how many bombs, causing how many torn limbs, how many shattered minds, originated here, at Pembrey Country Park.

27	28
24	**25**	26
	23	

Vale of Neath, Lampeter and Llandeilo Landranger sheets 146, 159, 170

VALE OF NEATH (CWM NEDD) AND OTHER VALLEYS

The Head of the Valleys Road descends to Swansea by the Vale of Neath. There is a Forestry Commission picnic place with three walks at **Glyn Castle**, *835 028*, overlooking the vale: turn off the A465(T) for Resolven, straight on at the war memorial and then bear left and uphill. The Melin Court Valley, Resolven, *825 017*, has a waterfall and oakwood, private but with a path from a car park on the B4434.

However, the vale, containing the trunk road, is rather a dismal corridor. The upper valleys of the Nedd and Mellte, with many waterfalls and limestone gorges, are within the

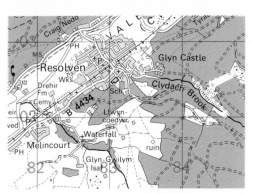

Brecon Beacons National Park and in what the Forestry Commission calls, confusingly, Coed y Rhaiadr (nothing to do with Rhayader further north). Turn off the trunk road for Glyn Neath, immediately taking the B4242 right for Pontneddfechan and after a mile or so the minor roads towards Ystradfellte. This junction needs care if you are not to be swept along to Dyffryn Cellwen.

Parking places are 1 mile south of Ystradfellte at *928 125* on the Mellte, or at Pont Melin-fâch, grassy with good deciduous trees, *907 105*, for the River Neath. Continue north of Ystradfellte 2½ miles (for Heol Senni) for an open picnic place by Afan Llia, *927 164*. Here we are really out in the air, and if only the sun will shine, what a relief!

The valley of the Mellte is beautiful and said to be neglected.

Dare Valley Country Park, 477 acres, is accessible on foot from Aberdare or by car via Cwmdare or Highland Place (B4277); the centre is at *982 027*. National Coal Board and British Rail lands have been reclaimed with the help of 20,000 trees from the Forestry Commission planted in 1973, the Year of the Tree. Moorland walks extend beyond the park.

CAIO FOREST, AND LAMPETER

Caio Forest Walk *679 405*, ♀ ♠, *2 walks, 1m each, FC*
Drive straight through the isolated village and bear left at the Forest Office. The car park is nice and the picnic site all that can be desired, near a bubbling stream. But where are the 'very attractive high-amenity plantations on land leased from the National Trust'? A few acres of red oaks was all I could find, and walking along the path to find the views of 'twelfth-century Caeo Church' I found my way barred by a fence. Two other paths also met the same fence. There was one marker, rather ambiguous. After a dull climb to the top of the valley side – it is almost a wall – I found a

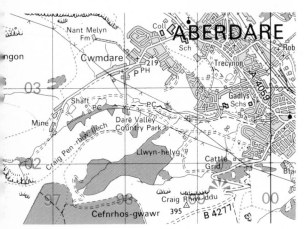

scattering of the original oak and bilberry; only enough to make one sad. The forest road here levels out and is old enough to have heather along it – an amenity, I suppose, in its way. I descended between the spruces in a fraction of the time it had taken to follow the graded forest road. I'm afraid it is all geared for production, and the red oaks are just a gesture. The other

walk 'meanders along the streamside with remnants of old natural oak'. Remnants is right.

Lampeter: Pantmawr *576 494*, ♀ ♠,
picnic place and walk, FC
The little forest is easily reached from Lampeter – it is about ¾ mile north of the town

Oak gives way to spruce in the Caio Forest

centre. It is a mixed wood where one might have spent happy hours playing Red Indians. There are enough dark stands of hemlock and spruce to give an authentic sense of being off the map, and some tall bracken and scrub for stalking in. Older trees are both conifers and Angiosperms. As a visitor I slightly felt I was trespassing. The wood is much walked in by local people – and long may it continue so.

There is another picnic place on the B4337 (leave by the A482) a mile north of Trefilan: a steep-sided cwm. I did not visit this, and I hope there are a few native trees.

Forest of Brechfa
This large forest south of Lampeter has several picnic places. There are views of very individual and intricate country with quiet roads and many old woodlands as well. Forestry is very much integrated with the landscape. There are miles of forest roads to explore. Four picnic places give access to the forest roads. Minor roads west from Llanllwnt

and north from Brechfa itself lead into the forest. Only about 12 miles from Carmarthen, this interesting countryside is little visited, and I shall certainly go back there when I have no schedule to make me hurry. Especially worth exploring is the valley of the Cothi.

NEAR LLANDEILO

By Llandeilo, which looks unbelievably pretty from across the river, is the ruined and romantically sited Dynevor Castle. There is also a new castle with its own private grounds, but the Castle Woods, overlooking the Tywi, are a nature reserve of 62 acres, reached by a gateway in the town. Tall wych elms are now being removed after Dutch elm disease has done its worst; oak will be planted.

Gelli Aur or Golden Grove 590 190, ♀ ♠,
99 acres, walks being planned, CP
The sadly empty grey school of Golden Grove faces a little decorative well, with an

Large ilex trees at Gelli Aur

inscription in barely Latinate capitals: 'DRINK AND BE THANKFUL'. Within the enormous park – much more than 99 acres – is a great Regency house, a fine ageing arboretum, a forest of young spruces, a farm with a large herd of Friesians. The mansion is now an agricultural college, and the grounds are open only during holidays. Out of season, I explored as much as I could without disturbing anything larger than a rather weary hedgehog, and without actually seeing the house. Keeping to the edges, one can stride out on a ridgeway path from the south-west corner (above the map reference) to enjoy a fine view and a quite enormous group of *Quercus ilex*. There are deer. Descending by a park roadway one can reasonably exit by the drive at the north-east corner onto the B4300 without intruding on the life of the college. Work is in hand and the precise functions of the Country Park are as yet not clear.

An important woodland reserve of the RSPB,

Gwenffrwd and **Dinas**, now totals 1723 acres. The hill of Dinas is wooded with oak and circuited by a nature trail. It is 12 miles north of Llandovery at *787 470*, near the Llyn Brianne Reservoir. The larger woodland of Gwenffrwd is protected, especially during the breeding time. A limited number of permits are available from The Lodge, Sandy, Beds SG19 2oL. Kites are frequently seen in winter, rarely in summer when they take to the moors. Sessile oak and downy birch are the dominant trees of the woods.

WALES & THE MARCHES
Brecon Beacons and Brecon Forest
Landranger sheets 160, 161

BRECON

Nine thousand acres here belong to the
National Trust, including most of the
mountains. Pen-y-Fan was given by the
Chairman of the Eagle Star Insurance
Company, Sir Brian Mountain; one wonders if
his physical stature was as great as his
generosity. Talybont Reservoir, heavily
surrounded with larch and spruce, but with
pockets of hardwoods, is a 350-acre nature
reserve. Wildfowl include pochard, tufted
duck, wigeon, goosander, Bewick's swan and
whooper swan.

North and west of Brecon are many woods
in the valleys.

Nature Reserves near Brecon
Pwll-y-wrach, near Talgarth, *164 328*, is a
small oak and ash wood with spindle and
dogwood, a nature reserve of 20 acres, with a
muddy track to a waterfall. You can park in the
lane south-east of the hospital. **Nant Sere**,
Cantref, *038 238*, is a stream with deciduous
woods 3 miles south of Brecon. The minor
road to the moors crosses over the A40(T) so
that you have to turn into the town and out
again due south from Bridge Street.

There are large 'Danger Areas' north and
west of Brecnock District: take OS sheet 160.

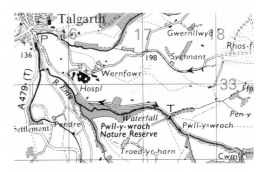

Gorse common at Ponde with the Black Mountains beyond

At **Ponde**, *110 365*, 6 miles north of Brecon, is a gorgeous gorse and birch common, with ponies – a good stopping place with a view of the Black Mountains. Bracken and thorn trees take over the rising ground at a clearly defined natural boundary.

Moorland and enclosed pastures alternate about the 1800-acre **Brecon Forest**, called Brycheiniog by the Forestry Commission. There are picnic places at *058 378*, 7 miles north of Brecon on the minor road to Crickadarn – fine beeches and a good view southwards – and at Battle Hill, *012 347*, 1½ miles north of Battle (turn right at Battle End).

Black bryony, Pwll-y-wrach, Talgarth

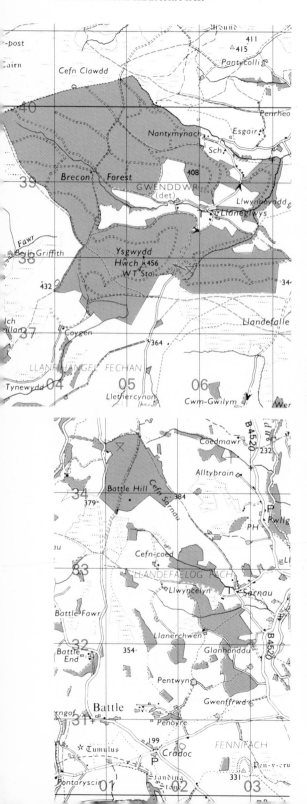

North of Merthyr Tydfil. Take the A470(T) for picnic sites and walks around Llwyn-on Reservoir, easy enough to find.

Below the reservoir and reached via the village of Cefn-coed-y-cymmer is the Forest Nature Reserve of Penmoelallt on the west bank of the Taf Fawr. The 17-acre wood on and below the limestone cliff is the home of

Sorbus leyana, known in this valley only. Extra specimens have been planted for study. The leaf rather resembles that of its close relation far away in the Isle of Arran. *Sorbus rupicola* grows large here, and there is a good range of lime-loving trees and shrubs.

Take the minor road north-east for Pontsticill at the interchange of the A470 and the A465(T). Three miles beyond the village the 'No Through Road' leads to Blaen Taf Fechan and Pont Cwm-y-Fechan. The Taf Fechan (*blaen* being merely a tip or leader) is fed from the mighty Pen-y-Fan, 2906 feet. Turn right at 'No Through Road', for, in ½ mile, Owls Grove Picnic Place – streamside, with waterfalls and a forest trail a mile or so beyond.

Ponies at peace in the woods at Taf Fechan

Pontsticill Reservoir: a wet morning

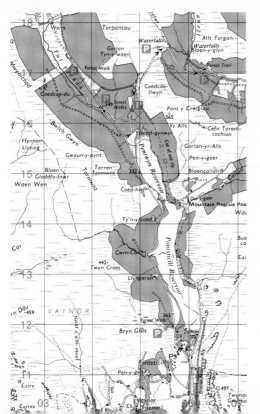

All these picnic sites and walks are close together beyond Pentwyn Reservoir. Close to Pontsticill is the Taf Fechan Forest Walk from *056 121*. I give no map references for the others and you would be unwise to go far without the Ordnance Survey sheet 160; on the latest edition the car parks are marked. The Pentwyn Reservoir, including $1\frac{1}{2}$ miles of disused railway track with scrub, is a nature reserve. Wintering wildfowl are the main interest.

Craig y Cilau *186 168*, ♀, *1m or more, very difficult, NNR*

Take the right fork upwards out of Llangattock and park just beyond the cattle grid. The 'Rock of the Retreat' is a limestone cliff: an awkward scrambling sheep track below it and very rough walking above. On the cliff grow native trees, among them lime and whitebeams. Two of these are found only in Brecon, one only at this place. They are distinguished only with difficulty from the common whitebeam, *Sorbus aria*, which also grows here, and are reached

TOP AND ABOVE: Craig y Cilau: a whitebeam in the rain

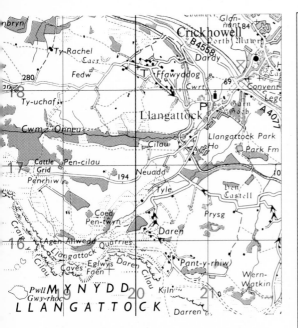

SORBUS TREES

The genus *Sorbus* is very widespread and various. From the five-lobed, plane-like leaf of the wild service to the toothed oval of the common whitebeam there is a whole spectrum of leaf shape, while the rowans' leaves are split into several pairs of leaflets plus a terminal one. Hybrids between rowans and whitebeams, none native here, show intermediate lobed/leaflet forms – a lesson in evolution.

The British whitebeams are a lesson in distribution, for many 'lesser' species or subspecies are local to western rocks from Avon through Wales and Lancashire to the Western Isles. Expert field botany is required to identify them.

All the *Sorbus* trees have pretty berries which can be made into good jellies. Best loved of all is the common rowan, often planted by Welsh cottage doors for its (white) magic – a sprig could be taken on any journey.

with even more difficulty. It is tragic that these rare trees should be at the mercy of the sheep if they dare to seed somewhere less inaccessible. Are we to suppose that the lesser whitebeams will only grow out of vertical cliffs? It is time to make sure that these little treasures can survive. No complex machinery of government needs to be brought to bear. All that is needed is a sheep fence: the minute loss of grazing could be made up by clearing a bit of bracken.

I'm afraid you will not enjoy the walk, but don't choose a rainstorm to do it in, as I did. I even lost my specimen of the most vivid red berries that you can imagine – not, I hasten to add, plucked by me, but by the wind. No pigment could ever match this colour, and the tree, *S. minima*, grows nowhere else in the world.

A beechwood of 57 acres, a National Nature Reserve, Cwm Clydach, *218 125*, lies close below the Head of the Valleys Road about a mile east of Brynmawr. Turn off at Clydach and head for Daren-felen. A leaflet from the NCC at Cardiff is highly informative.

Talybont Forest *064 170*, ♀ ♣, *trail 1¾m (steep), or shorter alternatives, FC*
Talybont has a charming stretch of tree-lined

canal. The reservoir is lined with magnificent large conifers and beeches: it would be well known if it were Cumbrian and not Cambrian. Up the valley, oaks take over for a mile or two, then the forest begins. The Forestry Commission parking ground seems carved out of the spruces and larches; generous and monastic, it could contain a crowd. But here, in this grand mountain valley, one may experience solitude. The trail takes in some waterfalls and viewpoints. The spruces are the not-too-alien Norway species, and there are many native trees, even a sweet domestic plum by a ruined wall. Streams flush out of the tree-

Oaks at Moccas Park

ABOVE: a waterfall on the Talybont trail, and BELOW: Craig y Fan Ddu, and the parking ground, Talybont Forest

clad slopes, frothing like brown ale, and lichens gleam in the grey light of yet another rainstorm.

At **Moccas Park**, *355 425*, the Black Mountains to the south seem far away in the rich, sheltered valley of the Wye. Moccas is a deer park, a surviving wood pasture. 'Every one of Moccas' ancient trees is a unique and irreplaceable monument. Those "gnarled, low-browed, knock-kneed oaks" are living records of centuries of interaction between natural growth and human work, and their like may not be seen again'. So writes Richard Mabey, quoting Francis Kilvert a hundred years before him. He mentions that three beetles are found here and nowhere else in Britain – also 97 lichens (but there are 202 at Melbury Park in Dorset).

This ancient park does not provide a woodland walk, unless you write for a permit to the NCC at Hereford, or Attingham Park, Shrewsbury. A good deal can be seen from the road, and my picture was taken through the fence while I stood in a patch of nettles.

WALES & THE MARCHES
The Forest of Dean and
the Wye Valley Landranger sheets 149, 150, 162

28	33	34
26	**11**	12
23	9	10

THE FOREST OF DEAN

⚥ ⚑, *285,000 acres, countless walks, many picnic sites, FC (National Forest Park)*

Like the New Forest, Dean was a royal forest before Domesday and remained under the Crown until taken over by the Forestry Commission in the 1920s. It is a rough, upland plateau of Old Red Sandstone bearing Carboniferous rocks which outcrop variously. Ridges of Mountain Limestone look over the deep Wye Valley to the west.

Between the Severn and the Wye the Dean is on the road to nowhere. It is full of coal and iron and the iron has been mined since Roman times or before. With iron below and deep forests of oaks, with deer, above, it continued a mysterious and self-sufficient existence for many centuries. The people were independent and unruly, the country covered with 'irregular tracks and horrid shade so dark and dreary as to render its inhabitants more fierce and audacious in robberies' – William Camden, 1607. Most of the foresters were miners, and to this day any man born in the Forest of Dean who has worked a year and a day in a mine has the privileges of a Freeminer, entitled to dig for iron ore or coal under licence from the Crown. The King's Gaveller once took a third of the profits: now the Deputy Gaveller at Coleford still grants the 'gales', and small two-man drift mines (along the 'drift' of the rocks) are still working for coal, all the major collieries being long since closed.

Between the thirteenth and seventeenth centuries over sixty forges were at work in the forest, some fixed, some itinerant, each using at least one oak tree a week as well as dead and dry wood. Coppices were maintained for charcoal for the fixed forges.

The Dean oaks were needed for the Navy and iron working was effectively stopped at least for a century after 1650. The Commonwealth Government attempted to replant some 16,000 acres: '400 huts belonging to poor people were thrown down. As a result

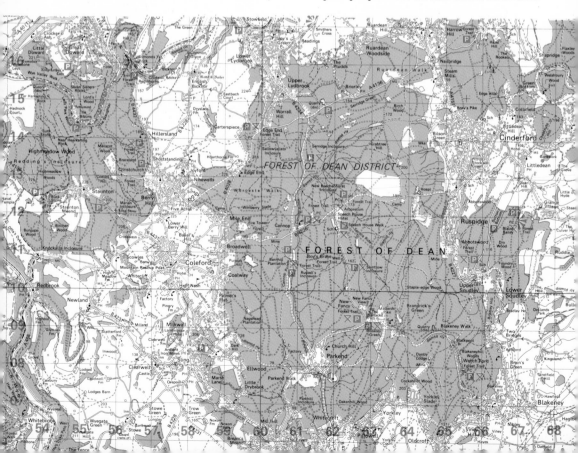

riots broke out . . . fences were broken down, cattle driven into enclosures and wood set on fire' – John Rogers, 1941. This struggle between government and people is a continuing story of the forest. Why did not the Crown take over the mines as it was often advised to do? The answer must be that 'free' is not an empty word. The miners, like commoners elsewhere in England, had rights extending back to 'Tyme out of Minde', as the miners' ancient charter puts it. They were Freeminers before there were any effective kings.

The Miners' Court, where miners took the oath on a stick of holly, was eventually moved to Speech House (*620 122*, finished in 1680) where also a Verderers' Court attempted to preserve the vert and venison. The court still meets four times a year. The forest was divided into six 'walks', each with a keeper and a lodge – one can be seen at Danby Lodge, *645 083*. Other lodges were destroyed by angry miners. Freeminers could sell their gales and 'foreigners' opened large collieries in the nineteenth century such as Trafalgar, New Fancy, Go On and Prosper, Strip and At It: by the 1920s they produced a million tons a year. Rent and royalties of the Dean mines in 1938 were £17,848. The last large pit closed in 1965. New Fancy's waste-top is now a Forestry Commission viewpoint. 24,000 acres are now under productive forestry.

The forest is very beautiful. The bold shapes of the scenery are further broken by quarries and mine workings and the woodlands are not made any the less interesting by the many trackways, from Roman pavements to disused mineral lines, and other signs and remains of human endeavour. The Forestry Commission's conifer plantations are not allowed to intrude, usually, on a foreground of open oak forest or beechwood, where commoners' sheep graze amongst the trees. The rugged topography tends to abrupt changes in soil and vegetation, and provides constantly changing, distant views of tree-clad hills.

The native oak is the durmast, but sessile oaks were planted for Navy timber. Only 200 trees were estimated to remain after one Sir

John Winter, with a royal grant in the seventeenth century, removed 30,333 trees.

There are many picnic places arranged along scenic drives and elsewhere and trails intersect at some points. All the waymarked Forestry Commission walks are over 2 miles.

The Scowles *606 046*, ♀ ♣, *200 yds, uneven and muddy, private but open*
There is no parking place to speak of on the road (B4231, Bream to Lydney), but there is a large lay-by ¼ mile to the south-east. Approached by a lane full of blood-red puddles are the gloomy caves – 'Scowles' – of ancient iron workings: a scene full of the atmosphere of a picturesque grotto with the added interest that it was a place of work. It is now overgrown with tall beeches and shattered yews, full of ferns, but with the dark red rock sculptured by the miners it is a great open wound of the landscape, bones exposed, flesh removed. You can walk south through the beeches to recover from this disturbing experience, but this wood is outside the Forest Park – it leads eventually to Lydney Castle.

Speech House Forest Trail *623 123*
The Court Room is now the dining room of the Speech House Hotel (obtain a trail leaflet here) and can be seen by non-diners at 'reasonable hours'. The trail (3 miles long, shorter route of 1¾ miles) includes an old inclosure, coppice chestnut, open oak country on sandstone, a reclaimed tip as a picnic place and even high-tension power cables. An ancient holly tree is said to have been planted for winter fodder. There is a picnic place amongst old oaks at stop 12. There is also a Spruce Drive planted mostly in 1900, of Norway spruces now tall and well bushed, and a lake made in 1974 for wildlife. It is fed by a brook and is surrounded by damp woodland with ferns and mosses. The arboretum, east of Speech House, with a fine shelter-belt of redwoods (not so tall as to be remote), includes many interesting and attractive firs and really lovely 'exotic' birches, with southern beech and most other specimens you would expect among 200 different species. The lay-out is informal, but the labelling of the trees is scrappy.

Wench Ford Forest Trail *655 080*
Short trail (3 miles) in mature oakwood, schools trail (3 miles) with mine workings, Forest Lodge of Charles II's time, geology notes in leaflets, 'grand old yew', railway sidings grown over and enormous pipe for stream made of old boilers. Longer trail (4 miles) is energetic with spectacular views.

Blackpool Bridge, $\frac{1}{3}$ mile north of the picnic site, is a former railway bridge over a minor road to Cinderford beside which, a few yards along, can be seen a section of an ancient paved roadway, the Dean Road, possibly Roman.

Edge End Forest Trail *597 142*
The large picnic site is set back from the main road, A4136, but unfortunately you have to cross the road to the trail. The leaflet, good on topography of views, is informative on trees (but not the Weymouth pine stand between stops 2 and 3) and birds, and notes three mine workings abandoned in 1960 but with equipment still in place. The mine is only 200 yards from the picnic site and well worth looking at. Complete trail $3\frac{1}{4}$ miles, shorter route 2 miles.

There are trails also at **New Fancy**

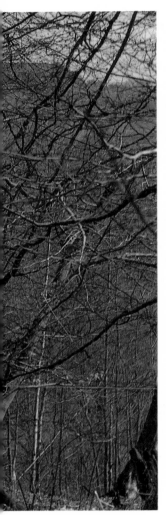

TOP: a Dean miner, ABOVE: The Scowles
LEFT: in the Forest of Dean, near Bream

viewpoint, *628 096* (parking for coaches), **Abbotswood**, *658 109*, and **The Wilderness**, *659 169*. This last has three loops and is largely concerned with non-woodland features, hot on geology and herbs: it even includes massive waterworks, more pylons, and boggy ground 'once the home of sundew'. The leaflet also includes a reading list.

Symonds Yat Forest Trail *565 160*
Everyone wants to see the rock and there is a charge for the coach and car park. Leaflet from a superb log cabin. Viewpoint over Wye.

Durmast oaks of all ages. Very small arboretum with 'lovely fir', *Abies amabilis*, trapped by honeysuckle into uncharacteristic bulges but still lovely. Dive in at the end of the trail near the road for this and an attractive young oakwood.

Buck Stone *542 122*
The Buck Stone is at 915 feet with distant views of the Black Mountains. It can be reached by a short walk from the end of a lane out of Staunton. From the post office turn right then left and fork right on to a dirt road

leading west. After the gate walk 500 yards then turn left through the older, open woodland to the rock.

For longer walks, 10 miles or over, see the Ramblers' Association leaflets. The more picturesque part of the forest to me is at the south-west edges near Bream and at the south-east around Wench Ford. There are other picnic sites with trails. I will only mention Boy's Grave: unhappily named, it is too muddy to be safe for cars in winter.

Mallinsons Veneer Mill at Lydney uses imported timber, the current demand in the furniture trade being for *Afrormosia* 'teak' etc, but there is also a demand for figured yew. All English yew is more or less figured, and supplies come from the Dean. The factory formerly used much local elm; so little valued was it that large squares of veneer were used for packing bricks, instead of straw.

LITERATURE

Baty, F. W. (1952) *Forest of Dean*, Hale, London
Edlin, H.L. (ed) (1963) *Dean Forest and Wye Valley Forest Park Guide*, HMSO, London

And many others: put in a 'subject request'.

From the Forest Bookshop, Coleford:
Jones (1981) *Walks in the Wye Valley and the Forest of Dean*, booklet published by the author.
Marfell, A. (1981) *Forest Miner*, published by the Forest Bookshop.

From the FC Office:
Leaflets for Forest Trails.
Visitors' Guide and map: refers more to the Wye Valley, lists addresses etc, but little help in the forest except that it summarizes the Forestry Commission trails.

Ramblers' Association leaflets: *Waymarked Paths Forest of Dean* and *Waymarked Paths Highmeadow Woods*.

An Ordnance Survey Outdoor Leisure Map (1:25,000) of the Wye Valley and the Forest of Dean is published in addition to the normal Landranger series.

THE WYE VALLEY

Highmeadow Woods seems to be the name used for several woods in a separate but joined western area of the Forest Park which was not administered by the Crown until 1817. The area includes Symonds Yat Rock and a great bight of the Wye in an 'incised' meander begun 600 feet higher than today. **The Christchurch Forest Trail**, *567 127*, 3½ miles, is described by the Forestry Commission as exceptionally interesting and varied.

There is a ferry at Symonds Yat – Yat means gate, and the river flows through the Yat dividing the village into west and east – and a footbridge at the Forestry Commission's Biblins Youth Centre from **Lord's Wood** to **Lady Park Wood**. Most of the woods in this section are of native trees.

Little Doward Wood *547 157*, ✦ ,
1m (seems like 3), rough, steep, dangerous in places, partly outside Forest Park
The rough-and-ready parking place indicated by the map reference is reached from Great Doward or the hotel at Little Doward and is close to King Arthur's Cave, and Lord's Wood and Doward Woods which are known for wild flowers. Some of the contents of this and other caves include extinct mammal bones, now in Monmouth Museum. Going downhill from the cave (to the right off the Biblins forest road), you can turn off right at a great beech root, full of lumps of native limestone, and pick your way by a little-used path through an ash and chestnut coppice up into beechwood. Soon you reach a massive limestone wall, which you may as well climb over where you can. Continue steeply upwards by the great, grey trunks of beeches, past their prime, and by bushes of spurge laurel to the limestone ledge above the Wye. Here grows a small-leaved subspecies of the whitebeam *Sorbus latifolia*. The largest tree grows very close to a yew – a curious habit of whitebeams, perhaps very easily explained by birds dropping seeds, but not so easily in view of the yew's heavy shade. One small tree grows up out of the crag itself, sheer above the river, and has mistletoe in it. There is ash and maple, with old hawthorns and ruined old beeches.

Rocks and whitebeam at Little Doward

An easier way to get here might be from the Doward Hotel, but you might miss, in spring, dog violets, wood sorrel, celandine, cowslips, spurge laurel, wood sage, stinking hellebore and green hellebore.

Follow the forest road towards The Biblins for the Seven Sisters Rocks and Lord's Wood, or continue across the footbridge for Highmeadow proper: this eventually brings you to Staunton, mentioned on page 45 for its Buck Stone.

Tintern, once a wire, iron, brass and tin plate centre, is best known for its Cistercian Abbey, largely thirteenth century, drawn by Turner and Girtin, and having had lines written some miles above it by Wordsworth – under a sycamore, of all trees. The Abbey is generally agreed to be best seen from between trees, being a little gaunt close to. The Forestry Commission has it between redwoods, which

does not sound appropriate even if the first trans-Atlantic cable *was* made at Tintern.

The road is lovely but obviously can be extremely congested in the summer time. The several walks from Tintern are easy to find. Another, the **Wynd Cliff and 365 Steps Walk,** starts from a small Forestry Commission car park, *524 973,* a waymarked nature trail somewhat confused with part of the Gwent County Council Wye Valley Walk. If you find the valley claustrophobic, turn uphill opposite the pub in Tintern and turn left and left again for the Fedw picnic site.

Fedw Woods *505 985,* ♀ ↟, *easy but rocky and ankle-twisting away from the forest road, FC*
The picnic site is high with glimpses of the Monmouth hills but sheltered by conifers and with a nicely crafted children's play area. The walk is easy enough for a semi-retired

Yorkshire terrier, who regarded it as *his* territory, and there are nice big Douglas firs, then cleared areas of larch with small oaks, gorse and mossy limestone lumps. There is an impressive pine-clad ridge, with beeches and a very fine view of the wide bowl in the hills of which Fedw is the southern side: opposite is Ravensnest Wood, which also I explored but found uninteresting in spite of some massive Douglas firs with offspring seeded along the

Picnic place, Fedw Woods

Wild daffodils in Dymock Wood

track side. But park at *504 000* for a dull walk by a loudly babbling stream, up a very gentle incline; good if you have a knotty problem to discuss with a friend.

NORTH OF THE FOREST

Dymock Wood *677 285*, ♀ ⚲, *about 1150 acres, 2 walks, easy, FC*
For wild daffodils, oaks, larches, beeches, ferns – especially daffodils – turn off the M50 at junction 3 for Gorsley, then left for Kempley, which also has crowds of nice, small daffodils, particularly in the churchyard. Unfortunately the M50 cuts through the small Dymock Forest, so choose your wood up-wind for less noise. **Hay Wood**, east of the road, is more charming, but nearer the road. **Queen's Wood**, to the west, is of maturing oak with yews under, the trail leading to Douglas firs and to wetland by a stream. It is an old forest but bears little sign of it.

Haugh Wood *593 365*, ♀ ⚲, *1000 acres plus, 2 walks, 1m and 2m, easy, NT, FC*
A silent hill with an old wood, once belonging to Hereford Cathedral, now partly coniferized. A good parking and picnic place, this is Hereford's local wood (take the B4224 east from Hereford, then the second left turning in Mordiford) and there are many footpaths and bridleways. Overlooking the Wye, snaking in its wide meadows, is a steep western outlier with footpaths from Fiddler's Green or Cherry Hill, Fownhope. This western arm of Haugh Wood is of oak self-promoted from coppice with large yews: here badgers, deer and rabbits are little disturbed, and there are stinking hellebore, bluebells, spurge laurel and elderberry. This last doesn't sound exciting except that it springs around the edges of the yews where the deer shelter and badgers excavate. I hadn't realized that spurge laurel was such a common plant until I came to the Wye.

At **Eastnor Castle**, *735 369*, near Ledbury, is an arboretum, open seasonally, where Atlas cedars date from 1847. North from here the Malvern Hills are a 40-square-mile Area of Outstanding Natural Beauty.

29	30	
27	28	
24	25	26

WALES & THE MARCHES
Mid Wales
Landranger sheets 135, 147

ABERYSTWYTH

The Rheidol and Ystwyth Forests, owned by
the Forestry Commission, provide a semicircle
of picnic places and walks within 15 miles of
the town. Closest, to the north-east, is Plas
Gogerddan, *633 838*, near an old estate with
oaks and redwoods – and rhododendrons. Take
the road for Penrhyn-coch from the A487(T) or
the A4159. Through Penrhyn-coch the small
road continues eastwards through the forest to
Llyn Pendam, where there is another picnic
place amongst the conifers, *708 839*. South of
this quiet place is Bwlch Nant-yr-Arian Visitor
Centre, at a viewpoint on the A44(T), with
bookstall, slide show and disabled facilities,
717 814.

Devil's Bridge, *742 770*, on the A4120, has
no Forestry Commission connections and is
heavily commercialized, but quiet enough out
of season. It is the end of the line for the little
Rheidol Railway with its sharply picked-out
Victorian lettering, and a viewpoint for the
curious patterns of local forestry on the wide
valleyside. The Nature Conservancy's Coed
Rheidol, an oakwood, is below. Two miles
south-east on the B4574 the largest planted
area of the Ystwyth Forest begins at The Arch,
a Forestry Commission picnic place, *765 756*,
with a trail, indicated by a dignified stone
archway memorial to George III's Golden
Jubilee, built by one Thomas Johnes, a pioneer
of upland forestry in Wales. Johnes planted
over a million trees, especially larch, before
1830, and also restored oakwoods depleted by
mining furnaces. There is a viewpoint to look
down Cwm Rheidol and to Pumlumon and
Cadair Idris if it is clear. Two miles further
south-east at Cwmystwyth begins the
mountain road down Afon Elan, quiet and
treeless for many miles above the gleaming
meanders.

The Arch picnic place is in the Ystwyth
Forest, which has two other picnic places
south-east of Aberystwyth. One is Black
Covert, *668 727*, near Trawsgoed (Crosswood)
Bridge, off the B4340. Here the trail leads to a
butterfly reserve. The other is further south
along the B road. Turn at a sharp bend onto a
riverside road to Pont-rhyd-y-groes – about ½

Forest and pasture, south of Machynlleth

The Arch in the Ystwyth Forest

Hawthorn on the cliff, Pen-y-graig

mile along is **Ty'nbedw**, *695 717*, with alders, and a walk which circulates in typical estate woodland, attractive and mature in a stream valley, then emerges into young modern forestry just to emphasize the difference. Chanterelles under the spruces turned out to be quite tasteless, probably because of the very wet weather.

Penderi, Llanychaiarn *554 735*, ♀, *20 acres, cliffside, NR*
Following the instructions in the *Nature Reserves Handbook* and in search of 'hanging oakwoods', took me to a hair-raising cliff via Pen-y-graig Farm, signed off the A487(T). This was an inspiring as well as an awe-inspiring walk in a chill October sunset, with the sea lathering over sinister dark rocks, too

From the picnic place in the Hafren Forest

far below to be audible. I found only some wind-blasted hawthorns; no oaks, which it seems are further north. I had turned south instead. The moral is, work out the position on the map beforehand. Fulmar, cormorant, shag and chough are to be seen here by those with a better head for heights than I have. The farmer courteously allows you to park. Note that there are two other Pen-y-graig Farms nearer to Aberystwyth – this one is 5 miles south.

Hafren Forest *856 868*, ♠, *walks 3–8m, mostly strenuous, FC*
Llanidloes is the nearest town, but Hafren is nowhere really, though a great forest and very beautiful. I suppose a few thousand oaks and alders had to be destroyed to make it, but probably less than for most. Here below Pumlumon Fawr (Plynlimon) some 8000 acres of very green trees maternally enclose the infant Severn or Hafren, no weakling, as, monitored by hydrologists using a variety of weird constructions, it gambols over the first 4 miles of its 200-mile journey.

The walk up the Severn, to its source if you wish, starts at a very pleasant stopping place with tables overlooking a meadow where Welsh ponies with Arabian connections pose daintily against the background of spruces. Old ash and sycamore trees survive from a former farmstead, difficult to imagine now. There are four other walks, but the map leaflet is due to be revised as I write. Note that the Severn, a mile or so upstream from the car park, is the right-hand branch of its tributaries Hore and Tan Llwyth, the path at present marked in

blue and yellow. Yellow markers continue to
the source above the tree-line at 2427 feet: this
is an 8 mile walk there and back, returning by
Pen Pumlumon-Arwystli.

The forest road north-eastwards makes an
impressive forest drive, emerging in moorland
pasture just above the almost unnoticeable
village of Staylittle. Continue a ½ mile north up
the B4518, and turn left for the shrunken
corpse of Dylife, a mining town now conserved
among heaps of grey spoil. Thousands of tons
of lead a year left here at one time – by
packhorse. Follow the mountain road, the old

The River Severn 4 miles from its source

route to Machynlleth, which was the mediaeval
Welsh capital, for a fantastic view of the hills,
so uneven and varied as to be almost ugly, and
shapes of Welsh forestry: great wedges, caps,
belts and gussets, under tumbling clouds and
vicious showers of rain. How green and smooth
are the pastures down below!

RHAYADER

Rhayader is a thoroughly nice place with good
woods and amazing forests. It is rarely visited
by tourists, even at the height of the season.
Hillside oakwoods hang above the road
southwards (A470[T]) and the mountain road
by Afon Elan, mentioned earlier, which
reaches into the Ystwyth Forest. These steep
woodlands make for uncomfortable walks, but
I will give the details, at least to enter and see
them: they are very consistent in character and
you may feel that exhaustive explorations are
hardly worth the effort. This is not to decry
their absolute value as nature reserves, as yet
unofficial.

Above Dderw *953 688*, ♀, *100 acres,*
fp, pf
Dderw, usually *derw*, is Welsh for oak. Leave
Rhayader by the B4518, immediately turning
right onto the signed 'Mountain Road'. The
wood is 1 mile up the valley. There is space to
park near the cattle grid. The road continues to
the Elan Valley.

Gwastedyn Hill *976 677*, ♀✹, *1½m,*
fp, very steep
The woods overhang the main road and the
Wye, and though it is possible to stop by the
roadside and start climbing, the footpath gives
a more gradual approach and good views. Park

Oaks at Dderw, Rhayader

near the lane which branches off left from the A470(T) going south only a $\frac{1}{4}$ mile out of Rhayader (or walk from the town). You pass the local workhouse, converted to a fine hotel, on your right, and the footpath is signed. It goes through three fields, all the gates of which must be closed of course, and by an ancient hollow-way, with hollies and ashes, up to the bracken moor and then into the top of the oakwood.

Tywi and Irfon Forests
North and north-west of Llanwrtyd Wells the Forestry Commission has a whole string of picnic places along the Irfon and the riverside road to Abergwesyn, notably at Crug, by the waterside, 4 miles from Llanwrtyd Wells, and others downstream. At a bridge over the Irfon stream, *836 556*, is the entrance to the Craig Irfon Reserve, 20 acres. **Nant Irfon** is the name of a much larger reserve 340 acres, which includes high oakwood with rowan, hazel and ash. This is a National Nature Reserve: a permit is required from the Regional Officer, NCC, Plas Gogerddan, Aberystwyth, Dyfed SY23 3EB.

In the very large central part of the Tywi Forest above Llyn Brianne a picnic place at Fannog, *815 500*, is the only one to offer a forest walk – a short one to a viewpoint over the lake. Turn off the A483(T) by Llandovery power station for Rhandirmwyn, then continue north for 8 miles; there are viewpoints also at Clochdu and Cwm Bys nearby. A northern plantation of the Tywi Forest is near Strata Florida, *745 657*; only about 15 miles from Aberystwyth by the B4340.

29 30 39
27 **28** 33
25 26 11

WALES & THE MARCHES
Radnor Forest and the Borders

Landranger sheets 147, 148

Coed Sarnau and **Abbeycwmhir**

042 705, (♀) ♣, picnic place, FC

This is an amazing landscape of hills, pointed or rounded, all with funny hats provided by the Forestry Commission. There are long drives through or beside the trees, and forest roads are open, visitors being scarce. Close to, the spruce forests are lacking in charm, but the wider vista is always compelling; and even wrecked undergrowth scattered with old fuel cans takes on a certain remote, melancholy character. Descend to the village of Abbeycwmhir – it has a post office shop, but this is no supermarket – and view the Abbey remains (Cistercian, sacked 1402) and the splendid Hall, its clear light-grey stone competing with a sugar-loaf hill covered with evergreens.

There is another picnic place, *085 612*, with more varied woodland at the **Shaky Bridge** on the Ithon, 1½ miles east of Llandrindod Wells. Turn off by the famous automobile palace. The town's lake has a small patch of oakwood on one bank, and an island with a resident heron – more than one, I hope – watchful, but not so shy as herons usually are.

Abbeycwmhir Hall and Sugar-Loaf Hill

Wooded slopes near Abbeycwmhir

Radnor Forest *205 638 (parking for NR)* ♣ ♨, *forest road, FC*

From Kinnerton, *244 633*, take the small road north-west towards the trees; turn left after ½ mile and continue up the gentle gradient of the forest road, ignoring a left and right fork and passing a stile on the left. After 2 miles you emerge into newly planted ground. A road turns left towards a radio mast. Park by the locked gate. The nature reserve's south-west corner is ½ mile along the fence, but is not marked.

As a woodland walk this belongs to the space age, but the view is slightly more than

hemispherical and the hills look primaeval, which of course they are. In poor visibility this is hardly worth the drive, merely to exchange the Forestry Commission's Sitka/willow herb/coltsfoot for the nature reserve's equally monotonous heather moor. Note, however, that inside the fence of the radio mast are many

Forestry road, with willow herb, Radnor Forest

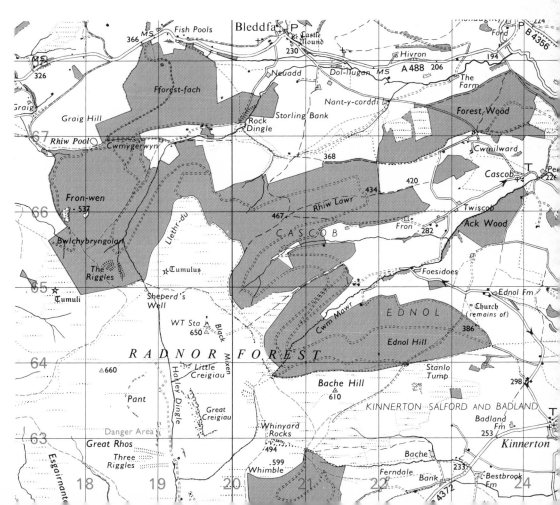

Looking east from the summit plateau of the Radnor Forest: clouds posing as glaciers

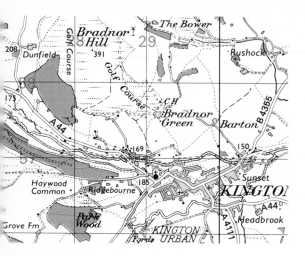

lowland weeds and good grass. Any year now there may be a birch or sallow seedling. The height is 2080 feet. The 'natural' state of the moor is the result of 5000 years of grazing.

HEREFORD AND WORCESTER

Bradnor Hill, *282 584,* is 340 acres of National Trust common, but there is a golf course on the top. Is this another example of an unfortunate affinity between commons and guided missiles? The steep west side of the hill is half occupied by a slab of the Forestry Commission's Radnor Forest.

A more interesting National Trust hill, part of 1385 acres attached to **Croft Castle,**

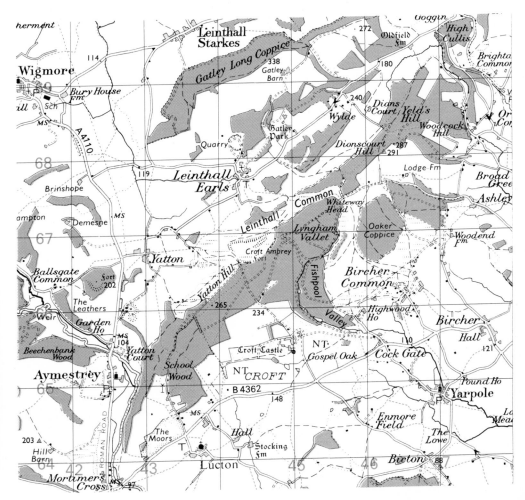

455 655 (avenues of chestnut, oak and beech), contains Bircher Common, appropriately capped by Oaker Coppice. Croft Castle has an arboretum with a great avenue of chestnuts.

In between is the handsome country of the Arrow and the Lugg, nearly every hill dark with trees and anciently fortified. The faces of Pembridge's half-timbered houses, under their paint, speak of the forest.

Pembridge, Hereford and Worcester

31	32
29	30
27	28

South and Mid Gwynedd

Landranger sheets 115, 123, 124

MACHYNLLETH

Cwm Cadian (Valley of St Cadfan), Dyfi Forest *751 052*, ⚲ ♠, *2m or less, forest trail, FC*

This is an award-winning forest trail, with good trees, good marker posts, a good car park and a leaflet which makes intelligent use of two colours. The car park is planted around with

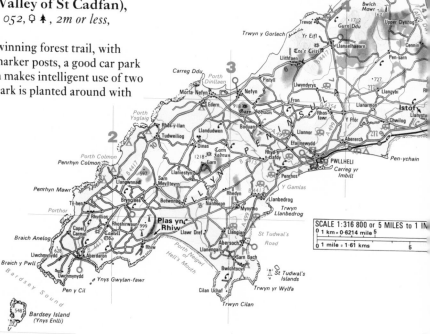

alders, a grand fir, beeches, cotoneasters, laburnum, a tulip tree and some cypresses. The walk is largely on the hillside above the cwm, with a detour to a small waterfall. Numbered posts are placed as guides, and numbers 6–10 are on a level forest road which forms a high terrace and a viewing platform for a display of perfect trees. These include unusual masses of Lawson cypress grown as a forest tree, with very well-formed, tall Sitka spruces in the foreground (south-east of post 6). The path rises through tall, dark Douglas firs into an equally dark beech plantation about forty years old – the trees were planted under oak coppice, some sad stumps of which remain. This is a severe loss of original character considering that the beeches are not impressive. One can climb beyond the forest road to the brow of the hill, admiring the cypresses, which form a wall of foliage on the

Cwm Cadian; a stand of Lawson cypress

outside of the planted group, unlike other conifers. Here on the mossy, gorsy bank is an old open beechwood, a truly poetic piece of landscape and a very unusual one in Wales. Larch and spruce are planted in the midst of its perfection, and its days are therefore numbered. A tiny corner like this could have been saved, surely, in this great forest of 30 square miles. It is not too late, if anyone heeds this plaint, for the conifers to be thinned prematurely, and this little patch kept as a nature reserve, while 35,000 tons of softwood in the forest around continue to crash to the ground every year.

Taking the road to Aberllefenni there is

Beech, and a woodland floor, Cwm Cadian

another car park beyond the interesting village of Corris at *770 093*, and a waymarked trail.

The **Nant Gwernol** walk (2 miles) starts from the station of this name on the Tal-y-llyn Railway, *682 066*.

Cadair Idris: Gaugraig *757 166, (♀)* ✿
If, like me, you prefer to approach large mountains cautiously and obliquely, turn down the by-road at the Cross Foxes Hotel junction of the A470/A487, east of Dolgellau. Turn left before Coed onto the moorland road. The large woodland to the north-west turns out to be coniferized, but there are lovely native oaks in the cwms. These give way to rowan and hawthorn as you climb to peer over Cadair Idris' left shoulder into one of his eerie, hollow spaces. Nothing much perhaps, but I stayed for ages sheltering under a wall from the sharp north-west wind, hoping for a gap in the clouds that never came, and, really, quite glad to get away from the enigmatic faces of alien conifers and the triteness of nature reserves. There is a slap in the face for ecologists here if one looks over an innocent-looking bit of wall marked as 'Old Quarry' on the map: there is a large heap of twentieth-century junk, including one or two cars. I rescued an oak picture-frame – it seemed symbolic in more ways than one.

HARLECH AND MAENTWROG

Native oakwoods remain in the pretty, upland country above Talsarnau and west of Trawsfynydd, at Coed Lletywalter (Woodland Trust, 94 acres, *600 275*), 3 miles south of Harlech, and at Coed Maentwrog. Lletywalter was scheduled as a National Nature Reserve but funds were not available and the Woodland Trust saved the day.

Above Talsarnau *629 372,* ♀ *, roads (notably at 626 364) and fps, private land within Snowdonia NP*
Take the steep, uphill road out of the village opposite the Ship Aground and Williams' Garage; either fork takes you to the same place, then you are on your own. You will find many marked footpaths, and, at the map reference, the nicest place to stop that you could imagine,

Perfect Sitka spruces at Cwm Cadian

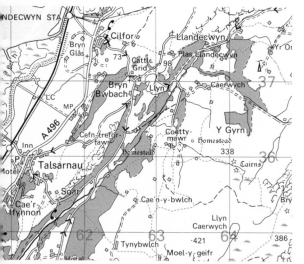

by a small lake. Lichen on stones and trees is a joy in itself, and sessile oaks, mostly quite small, are in every sort of shape. Northwards the little hills become even prettier, if that is possible, but the views are sadly polluted by pylons. Woodland to the north-east, towards Maentwrog, is mostly coniferized.

Coed Maentwrog *665 413, ♀, 2m nature trails and paths, 169 acres, NR, NT*
The wood is spread irregularly along the steep north side of the Vale of Ffestiniog, the river meandering below. Maentwrog is a small place, hidden amongst trees. The vale is dominated by a grandish hotel, but there is a pleasant pub, with good food, in the narrow street where the A496 heads south. The Ffestiniog Railway runs above the wood and a nature trail starts

Harlech Castle from the little hills above Talsarnau

from Tan-y-bwlch Station (35 minutes from Porthmadog) or from a car park, *651 416*, at Llyn Mair close by. The reference given is convenient for the middle of the wood, but parking is extremely limited on the roadside.

This is officially described as a 'relict valley oakwood'. There are many fine, large oaks as well as rowans and birches. There is too much bracken in places, and not as much natural regeneration as one would have hoped; but this is a good woodland walk by any standard. The little trains hoot beguilingly, and echoes confuse the ear. There are also supposed to be nuthatches, pied flycatchers, redstarts and warblers, none of which I saw, as usual.

TRAWSFYNYDD: COED-Y-BRENIN FOREST

Between Dolgellau and the Lake of Trawsfynydd is the Coed-y-Brenin of the Forestry Commission, with a Visitors' Centre at Maesgwm, *715 276*. This was closed when I approached and I'm sorry to say that I did not try the forest walk from the picnic place at the old Pont Dôl-gefeiliau, nor the one from the Ty'n-y-groes car park 3 miles south, nor did I, to my shame, examine the Forestry Commission arboretum at Glasdir, 1 mile east of Ty'n-y-groes. Instead I drove up eastern side of the wide Trawsfynydd Vale, obsessed with the mountain views and the ever-changing light. I drove, or was blown, into a peaty hole and had to be hauled out by a kindly giant called T. D. Jones. The twin towers of the power station gleamed at the end of this extraordinary avenue of hills like a distant castle in a Turner watercolour, and all around the hills the widely scattered, dark plantations of Coed-y-Brenin fitted snugly into the view.

The Forestry Commission maintains 50 miles of footpaths here, and it was ungrateful of me not to set foot on any of them. Oaks remain beside a mile or two of the very smooth A470(T) in the Afon Eden, and especially at Coed Ganllwyd, *723 243*, a National Nature Reserve of 59 acres.

Oak tree, Talsarnau

Coed-y-Brenin Forest; Cadair Idris in cloud in the distance

IN THE MOUNTAINS

Aberglaslyn *597 462, ♀, 1½m of riverside (easy), NT (517 acres)*

Here is the first view of Snowdon, or its head of clouds and its southern rampart, Yr Aran. Beautiful trees of somewhat mixed origin lean over the crashing white waters of the Glas. The path follows the track of an ancient railway, through its dripping, short tunnels and on to Beddgelert. You can shorten the walk by crossing the old railway bridge, now a footbridge, and returning by the road. The rather bare bank which rises very steeply 600 feet or so above is gradually being invaded by rhododendron, so the effect is distantly

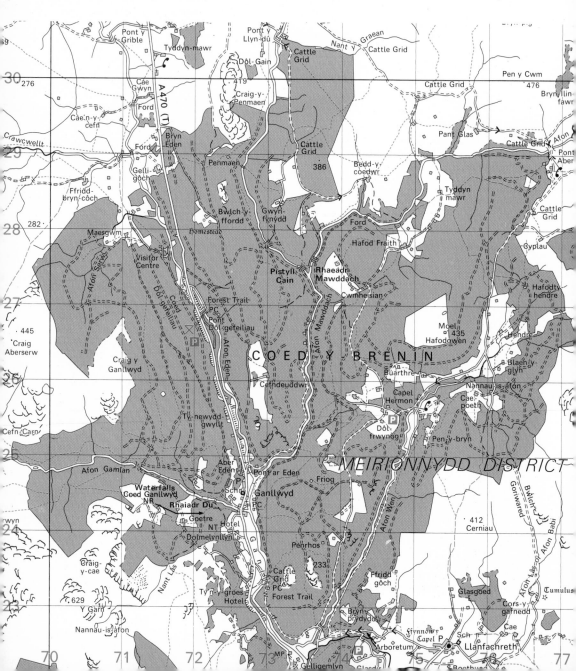

Tibetan. *Rhododendron ponticum* is not of course Tibetan, but the idea is there. It didn't look very nice, but if it helps to prevent erosion we can't complain. Perhaps one day the hillside will be clothed in oaks – the natural succession from rhododendron scrub, if any, is as yet uncharted so far as I know. But it is a well-known weed of Snowdonia.

The Lleyn Peninsula

On the Lleyn Peninsula the Forestry Commission has the Istof picnic place at Llanystumdwy, *468 386*, with a short walk in varied woodland, including old beeches, and, 1 mile north of Llithfaen at *354 444*, a short walk with good views from this north coastal hilltop near Yr Eifl.

Plas yn Rhiw Estate is 416 acres about a National Trust restoration of an ancient manor which became derelict in the nineteenth century; wild country with some trees down to the shore in places, but access on foot only. The map reference is *237 282* for the manor house.

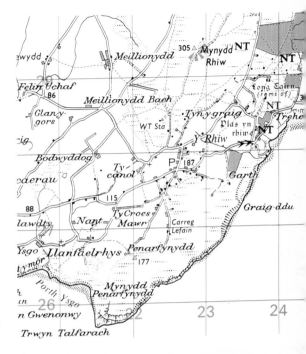

Aberglaslyn, the walk

Trees at Aberglaslyn

The Central Borders

Landranger sheets 125, 126

WELSHPOOL

Powis Castle *215 064*, ♀ ♠, *parkland,*
1m of driveway only, NT
Just in Wales, the pink, stone castle is worth
seeing on any account, and is surrounded by
fine trees. In the gardens (open seasonally) are
large silver firs and sequoias, and *Populus
lasiocarpa*, a Chinese tree with very large leaves
and pretty chains of fruits. At any time of the
year you can walk across the park by the main
drive and admire well-shaped old oaks and tall,
very tall, Douglas firs – over 180 feet.

Wellingtonias, *Sequoiadendron*, seem to fill
the wide Severn Vale at times, and the view
could be wonderful without Welshpool's
awkwardly placed gasworks. On the east side is
Leighton Hall, *242 046*. This is the home of
the Leyland cypress, the gardener's friend,
which emerged from the chance crossing of
two western American trees, the Monterey
and Nootka cypresses, in about 1888. Though
the hybrid has grown taller elsewhere, it is nice
to see it here, in an architectural setting that, to
say the least, emphasizes its purity of form.
One can walk through the grounds at weekends
– less than $\frac{1}{2}$ mile. The house is now a college.
(*Cupressocyparis leylandii* is over 100 ft in Devon.)

Powis Castle, from the footpath which is open all year

Earl's Hill, Pontesbury *407 057,* ♀*, 105 acres, 2m, fps, NR*
Earl's Hill rises to a craggy 1047 feet, an outcrop of some ancient volcanic rock. In the scree on the south-east side a thicket of ash makes a startling effect. There are sessile oaks and some large-leaved lime. Old thorns on the grassy northern slope lead to the reserve centre, housed in an old barn – a hillside of larches beyond. Pontesford Hill belongs to the Forestry Commission and is coniferized, but bordered by large sycamores, old yews and some nice firs.

Turn off the A488 at Alexander and

Cypress and stonework at Leighton Hall

Winter trees near the Barn, Earl's Hill

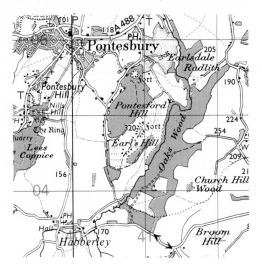

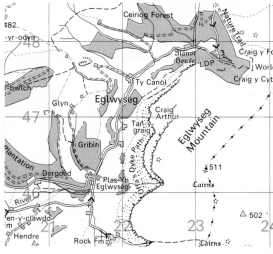

Ash thicket, Earl's Hill

Duncan's Garage. You are supposed to park here, but you may find a niche where the footpath is signposted 'To the Barn and the Reserve', if you follow the single track road.

CHIRK

Ceiriog Forest

Picnic places at *174 382* and *165 384* are in the forest proper. The Forestry Commission's Nantyr Walks are a series of easy waymarked walks, and the World's End Walk, under the cliffs of Eglwyseg Mountain, $1\frac{1}{4}$ miles, is laid out by the North Wales Naturalists' Trust, *243 477*. This mountain is a limestone cliff, in the chain which extends from the Great Orme.

Yews at Overton, near the Dee, were once one of the Seven Wonders of Wales, in what used to be Flint.

Ash keys are produced in abundance. They can be pickled when green for salads, according to John Evelyn, 1664.

73

31 32
29 30
Snowdonia and Anglesey

Landranger sheets 114, 115, 116, 124

SNOWDON

From Beddgelert you have the choice of two passes, west or east of Snowdon. The mountain itself has no woods, but it produces an annual rainfall measured in feet rather than inches (over 13 feet), and since most of this comes from the west you may be influenced by the weather in your choice of route. The right-hand pass, Nantgwynant, leads to the head of the Llanberis Pass, and Llanberis is the popular Snowdon playground, with railway connection to the peak itself, several nature trails and a Country Park, **Padarn**, of 320

grey when I visited this south-east cwm, but small oakwoods above the pass are extremely rich and beautiful, though well grazed by sheep and therefore unlikely to perpetuate themselves. On the opposite side of the road are the extensive plantations and green fields of Plas Gwynant.

acres, *584 606*. This manages to live alongside a massive hydroelectric scheme and includes the largest slate quarry in the world (which ceased operation twenty years ago), as well as the surviving native oakwood, Coed Dinorwic, which is a local nature reserve. Compared with the very moving story of the Dinorwic Quarry Hospital, the drama of the oakwood may seem slight. An excellent booklet gives a good account of both. All the attractions of Lake Padarn, including the railway, are seasonal, April to September, but the Country Park is open every day to walkers.

Nantgwynant: an oak walk *628 506*, ♀, *very steep, length optional, fp, NNR*
Real walkers take the Watkin Path, striding up by waterfalls and the ruins of the incredibly gloomy South Snowdon Quarry to the summit ridges, here to look down to lonely Glaslyn – *glas* meaning green, silver or blue, a versatile word such as English cannot aspire to. All was

74

Dulas

Llyn Gwynant
OVERLEAF: start of the Watkin Path up to Snowdon

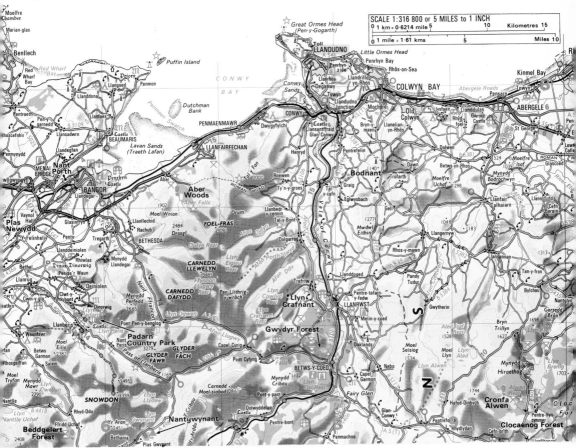

The parking place is a large roadside one with decent facilities. Cross the bridge where a daily weather report gives the cloud ceiling as well as other, perhaps more predictable, factors. A gap in the wall leads to a short, stiff climb through the richly lichened trees, or you can follow the Watkin Path as far as the waterfall and the adjacent Coed-yr-allt, also oak. A nature trail is marked on the Ordnance map but I couldn't find it; perhaps it is more obvious in summer, or perhaps it applies to the Forestry Commission walk which starts from a picnic place at *634 513*, a 'steep climb through rhododendrons and magnificent forests to a fine view' – not an attractive proposition on a wet, dark morning, though the view is sure to be worth the walk on a fine day.

Beddgelert Forest *574 508*, ♀ ♣, *various walks, campsite, wayfaring course, FC*
If you choose the uncluttered and very scenic Beddgelert to Caernarfon route – or better the opposite way in the afternoon with the sun behind you – you enter the central part of the Beddgelert Forest, which includes Nantgwynant to the east and Lleyn to the west. The car park and picnic place given above is at Pont Cae'r-gors (Glan y Gors) where start 'extensive systems of walks leading to viewpoints of Snowdon and Moel Hebog'. With all this wonderful mountain scenery about one does not want to plunge amongst the musky spruces, but the walks are there, and with fine silver firs to start you off.

The large campsite $1\frac{1}{2}$ miles south is extremely nicely situated, with 300 pitches in varying degrees of seclusion amongst attractive birches, oaks and alders; open all the year round with reduced facilities in the winter. A short forest trail and the wayfaring course start here.

BETWS-Y-COED

Betws, where Telford's Waterloo Bridge takes his A5 over the River Conwy, waits to sustain the traveller, even on Sundays, and to lure him into the forest. It is difficult to imagine Betws-y-Coed before 1920, when certainly it was wooded, and the hotels put up a few gaitered and flap-hatted walkers to the Swallow Falls (on the unpronounceable Llugwy) and famous climbers practised on Snowdon and Tryfan while planning to bag Everest or Annapurna.

Betws means an oratory or a chapel, *y-Coed*, in the woods, but *capel*, as at Capel Curig nearby, is a chapel, and it is perhaps the rushing waters that sing here. It is a tourist centre, but an umbilical centre too for the mountains, forests and rivers, and you feel the pressure of their immensity around you – or perhaps it is just the mildness and dampness of the sheltered air.

Part of the Beddgelert Forest and Llyn Cwellyn

The Information Centre, however, close to the station, is cool and orderly, and has intriguing exhibition panels with subtly lit still life of forest objects describing several local forest walks, lovingly gathered live samples of forest trees – and even samples of wood that you can handle, supplied by Henry Venables Ltd, Stafford. Good pocket folders, containing, in all, twelve walks leaflets, are available.

This is the **Gwydyr Forest** (20,000 acres, including 7000 acres of grazing and farming land). The story of its planting with every sort of forestry tree on sometimes the most difficult of ground, the fighting of fires by the railwayside, and the constant battle to keep out the sheep, is told in unselfconscious detail in the very moderately priced *History of the Gwydyr Forest* by Donald Shaw of the Forestry Commission (booklet no 28).

Local walks start from the car park at Pont-y-Pair, and for starters make for this. The B5106, the alternative route to Llanrwst, leaves the A5(T) by the bridge, Pont-y-Pair. Turn left *immediately* for the car park, *792 568*, and for

the minor road, which bumps around a triangle of land with Trefriw at the apex, and the Ugly House (Ty-hyll, *756 576*, an unmistakable landmark on the A5) at the west. This uneven plateau with its associated valleys, and Llyn Crafnant on its north-west side, is varied and ruggedly pretty, closely woven with trails, walks and forest roads. Artists' Wood, tall beeches done by Cox and others, is on the south side of the A5 with a disabled trail starting opposite the Miners' Bridge, a footbridge at *780 569* just along the road from Pont-y-Pair, while the minor road itself runs into the plateau along the Llugwy Valley on the opposite side, through immense Douglas firs. Almost as tall above the Ugly House are hemlocks on a boulder-strewn hillside; a glimpse of a giants' countryside.

A forestry exhibition is at the Visitor Centre and Forest Office near Llanwrst (**Gwydyr Uchaf**, *790 612*), and from here Lady Mary's Walk runs up by degrees to give good views of the Conwy Valley and, in autumn, a splendid array of woodland fungi. Some of the

Western hemlock, *Tsuga heterophylla*, Ty-hyll near Betws

viewpoints are now obscured by new trees; old beeches remain, but the walk is somewhat dark and sad. Lady Mary was presumably of the distinguished Wynn family whose estate forms the basis of the Forestry Commission lands.

Llyn Crafnant *757 621, ♀ ♣, 3m or much less, easy, FC*

The lake is separated from, and to the north-west of, the main part of the Gwydyr Forest by the road system, which joins the valley at Capel Curig to the south-west or the next valley to the south-east, containing Llyn Geirionydd. Take an uphill road out of Trefriw, leaving the cemetery on your right. The road is lined with woodland oaks and there are various places to stop, but the walk begins from a fine car park just below the lake, and there is a map displayed. The walk around the lake uses the tarmac road, a farm track, a footpath and the forest road through Douglas fir, Japanese larch and spruce, planted about 1937 and therefore mature.

Alternatively, the forest road going east from the car park then turns to follow the lakeside road, climbing about 250 feet before turning away to cross to Llyn Geirionydd. After a boring slog, it does give you a fine view of the picturesque crags of the head of the valley, where are remains of native oakwood.

Don't miss, at the first turning of this forest road, crossing the stile to a ruined lead mine, where a stupendous cave shelters, dripping a

Male fern, Crafnant

bit, the gold lichened stonework of what must have been cattle stalls or stabling, now occupied by magnificent ferns. The male fern may be the commonest (after the common brake) but in this dark and sheltered place, with the extraordinary coloured walls, its beauty is absolute. Was the world once all like this, dark, still and damp, when these precursors of the trees evolved?

Out in the wind the careful stonework of the mines above the green valley survives amongst the screes of spoil colonized by birches. There is no sign of mechanization in this lonely work-place. Note that the scree is dangerous and in any case should not be disturbed.

The famous gardens of **Bodnant**, 97 acres, National Trust, *803 721*, are on the east side of Afon Conwy 6 miles downstream.

BANGOR

Nant Porth *567 720, ♀, 19 acres, fp, NR*
This small ashwood on a limestone cliff is about a mile from the centre of Bangor and is in sight of the Menai Bridge. Turn off the A5(T) by a tyre service garage, next to Normal College, and drive around the sports field – Normal hockey girls may be seen. There is a car park at the end of the lane. *Sorbus porigentiformis* grows here, not as remarkably different from its very near relation *Sorbus aria* as its awful name might lead you to expect, but beautiful in leaf and in berry. Like other lesser whitebeams, it seems to survive by being difficult to get at. There is a pretty little bay willow and plenty of burnet rose, but too much sycamore. The path has been made up with timber steps.

Aber Woods (Coed Ydd Aber) *664 719, ♀ ♣, trail, 1½m or 3m, leaflet, NR*
Aber, meaning mouth, is a village 4 miles along the Strait, east of Bangor on the A55(T). The farm here belongs to Bangor University, which incidentally has an honours degree course in forestry. The parking place for the nature reserve is nearly a mile along the only by-road, and there is also a Forestry Commission car park, open in the summer. The trail is fairly

basic stuff, but the valley has a great number of Iron Age and Bronze Age remains, where evidence has been found of birch woodland up to about 2000 feet. The longer trail includes a hut circle, cairns and hill fort, and part of the Forestry Commission's 350 acres of spruce and larch. The plantation borders onto the nature reserve woodland and interpenetrates with original oakwood. The Forestry Commission might have left these fragments of oakwood alone, allowing regeneration behind their sheep fence; but no, they have planted larches in between. If they thought that old oaks are just sentimental why did they bother to plant a row of seven *Populus trichocarpa* on the reserve boundary? What sort of sentiment is that? At least the conifers make a neutral background. On the mountainside above, an arm of the conifer plantation reaches to a giddy height. This we can and must admire.

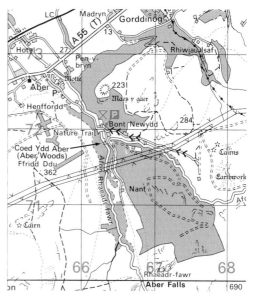

Alders in Aber Woods

The chief interest here for me is a fine alder swamp. The Welsh for alder grove, *gwern*, also means a meadow; a revealing synonym. Alder coppices were common once in the north Welsh valleys, the trees sold to itinerant makers of clog blanks and sweeping-brush heads. The clogs were finished, and worn, in Lancashire. Alder wood is light and water-resistant, and might still have its uses, but the trees do tend to occupy valuable meadowland, while the much less resistant softwoods can be grown on soil that is no use for anything else.

This little wood of maturing coppice trees has a distinct atmosphere, and it is a valuable piece of conservation. However, it is grazed by sheep, and I would plead for their exclusion, for obvious reasons, from at least part of it.

The nature trail leaflet draws our attention to the rich lichens of the trees, indicating unpolluted air – and so the air should be, only 2 miles from the sea. But we should be grateful that Irish industry is not developed enough to produce the acid rain that our own industry sends – on the prevailing wind – to Scandinavia.

CLOCAENOG FOREST, WEST

Cronfa Alwen *949 539*, ✦, *Visitors' Centre and forest walk, FC*
Turn off the A5(T) at Cerrigydrudion, onto the B4501. Turn left after Pont yr Alwen (2 miles north). The large clean-lined Alwen Reservoir fills the valley, where lie submerged the non-too-fertile fields of a farm whose buildings are now restored as an exhibition room and a shelter. The walk of 1 mile is marked out. If you don't walk even a mile the place is worth visiting for the groves of really lovely grand fir along the drive (and the walk). The small exhibition is good, except for crudely primitive paintings, and it makes the point that this very peaceful place is only 30 miles from Liverpool (or even less from Birkenhead, which takes its water from here). Fishermen stand rock-like by the water's edge.

There are 1800 acres of trees spread each side of 4 miles of the road northwards, and an even larger reservoir on the right hand side, Brenig. The vistas of bluish verdure are inspiring, even when it is raining.

Clocaenog Forest and Cronfa Alwen

SNOWDONIA NATIONAL PARK

Snowdonia is *Eryri*, land of the eagles, and Snowdon Mountain is *yr Wyddfa*. The National Park, 837 square miles, is the second largest in Britain. It contains the Gwydyr Forest, 19,473 acres, and Beddgelert Forest, 3000 acres belonging to the Forestry Commission. There is almost unlimited access to the forests, as well as a dozen waymarked walks, wayfaring courses, a campsite, many picnic places and two observation rides.

In the Llanberis Pass is an important Country Park, Padarn, and there are many nature trails of varying degrees of specialization. Even the power station of Trawsfynydd has a nature trail. Betws-y-Coed can be taken as the main entrance to Snowdonia, and the information centre is comprehensive.

Less obvious, but very important elements of the National Park are the large tracts of mountain country owned by the National Trust, and a range of different habitats, including several oakwoods, controlled by the Nature Conservancy Council: National Nature Reserves. The National Trust Information Centre is 2 miles south of Betws on the A5(T). The NCC (Cyngor Gwarchod Natur) for North Wales is at Plas Penrhos, Bangor, and a leaflet summary is available. Local nature reserves are controlled by the North Wales Naturalists' Trust (Ymddiriedolaeth Naturiaethwyr Gogledd Cymru Cyf) 154 High Street, Bangor.

Snowdon itself is in a National Nature Reserve of 4000 acres and ranging from 200 feet above sea-level in the lower Nantgwynant to the summit at 3560 feet. Considerable sums are spent on maintaining the famous footpaths – the Miners Track, the Pyg Track and the Watkin Path – to avoid further erosion. Cwm Idwal, nearly 1000 acres, was the first nature reserve in Wales. Cadair Idris Nature Reserve, at the south of the National Park is again nearly 1000 acres. Comparatively small woodlands are parts of these reserves. Of these Coed Tremadoc is precipitous; Coed y Rhygen, on the west shore of Trawsfynydd, is wet and mossy, with birch; and Cwm Glas Crafnant has 5 acres of woodland on lime-rich volcanic ash (not oakwood but ash, with hazel and hawthorn). All these three are not available without a special reason to visit and written permission.

The National Trust owns woodland at Llechwedd, near Harlech, and at Llyn Mair. The Maentwrog and Ganllwyd woods are leased to the NCC. South of Betws the National Trust has 25,820 acres of hills and valleys, mostly west of Ysbyty Ifan village and above the high Llyn Conwy. Near Capel Curig the Trust owns Llyn Idwal and the mountains Carnedd Dafydd, Tryfan, the north slopes of the Glyders and the north-west slopes of Carnedd Llewelyn: 15,800 acres altogether. There is a great deal of private land in the National Park and access is not automatic. Farmers on the whole are sympathetic, even very sympathetic, to the needs of walkers, but they do complain of broken walls and fences. Many visitors assume, naturally enough, that a National Park is land belonging to the nation. In fact all that National Park status means is that certain administrative powers exist (and are dealt with by a National Park authority) to survey and provide for public access for open air recreation in 'the countryside' or in 'open country'. The countryside is not defined and there is, of course, no such thing as open country. The control of visitors has become as important as providing access.

At the eastern 'gateway' to the National Park, on the A5, is the Conwy Falls nature trail. This is an object lesson in private exploitation of the countryside. The car park is rather larger than the area covered by the trail. A large, peeling building contains a café (closed) and a turnstile (not working) through which visitors must file and pay to see the falls. Nothing can destroy the beauty of the waterfalls, but the trail, staggering between points of very limited interest, is faced by the embankment of the main road, where a good deal of rubbish is tipped. The photographs you take have all the atmosphere of wild country; wild water, dark, rugged rocks, native trees – but they are lies.

Afon Machno from the A5 at the north-eastern gateway to the National Park

Conwy Falls

Pylons spoil the view 2 miles from Maentwrog, the National Park Centre.

Monotonous, virtually impassable and poor in habitat: spruce plantation 3 miles south of Betws in country that is a National Trust stronghold within the National Park.

ANGLESEY

There are virtually no old woods in Anglesey, charming though the island is in other ways. About Beaumaris there are many trees, and a small wood in Llangefni behind the church – **The Dingle** (just as ridiculous in Welsh – it is a *pant*) *459 759* – has pretensions to being an ancient oakwood. There are some oaks climbing a rock, but many sycamores and some old beech, with beneath them a great deal of policeman's helmet, hardly suggestive of great age, since it is the Himalayan balsam. The wood also includes a railway, a dirty river, and a meadow which, when I saw it, harboured a fat, white bull and a fat, white cow.

Newborough Forest *406 635*, ✦ , *1800 acres, forest roads, trail, FC*
Two miles beyond the village, signposted 'To the beach', is a splendid large car park which must be the Forestry Commission's best. It is elegantly formed of pools of tarmac amongst

the pine-clad dunes, where slacks known as winter lakes will not support trees. Newborough Warren is the best known of Anglesey's several dunelands, permanently shifting and with marram grass as the dominant vegetation. A whole village, Rhosyr, is supposed to be buried in the sand; one old house has been uncovered and forms a feature of the short trail. Green meadow grass grows where once was a floor of beaten clay.

The warren, or the half of it which is not planted with trees, is a National Nature Reserve and can fairly be said, botanical interest apart, to be quite unlike anywhere else, if only because of its wonderful simplicity against the background of the Snowdon mountains, crowned with clouds. I cannot say whether it was right to sacrifice even the more established part of this landscape to softwood production. Certainly the forest offers human comfort in a place where the nearest thing to a tree is the sometimes knee-high creeping willow – some still competing with grasses on

Newborough Forest

the dunes, in forest rides and even in the pasture further inland.

The foresters have planted many incidental bushes and trees, as if determined to create a garden of trees, rather than replace the monotony of the warren with the monotony of the Corsican pine. I found a horse-chestnut which will one day suppress the pretty and local variety of round-leaved wintergreen which was shining in the grass like a constellation of sad stars in the endless dark corridors of pine. Sallows, which grow here naturally, are supplemented by osiers and poplars from the nursery garden. There is even a bamboo.

By the road can be seen the richer green of *Pinus radiata*, which grows quickly but not always straight. Lodgepole pine is also used further inland, near a much less formal parking place, *412 672*, on the road to Aberffraw. Here the view outwards is only of saltmarsh and sea, while the sun sets over Wicklow and Kilkenny to the slow chiming of bells, the fluting of

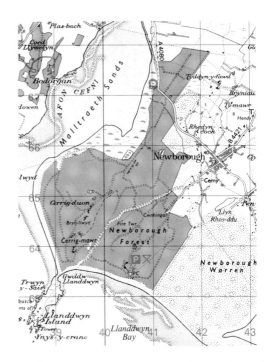

Round-leaved wintergreen, Newborough Forest   Bright green Monterey pine, Newborough Forest

Plas Newydd stables

organs and the crooning of tenors. There is fish-
and-chips just down the road at Malltraeth –
sounds Irish!

Plas Newydd *521 692*, ♀ ♣, *169 acres, parkland, NT*

There is a 73-acre woodland adjoining, under
covenant to the National Trust, but the prim,
Gothic beauty of the stables and a fine row of
Lawson cypress cultivars may attract you for
themselves alone, especially as this is an
unspoilt part of the Menai Strait. The artist,
Rex Whistler, adding a sharp Italian theme,
did a famous mural here, but slightly spoilt the
symmetry of the house with his plan for an
extension. There is a Rex Whistler room.
Wyatt and his assistant Potter did the original
Gothic around an old house, and Repton,
coming along later, advised planting a clump to
stop the stables upstaging the house. His
screen of trees is still there, and the stables are
perfect, with a dolmen on the lawn and
Snowdon beyond, across the water.

Clwyd
Landranger sheet 116

CLOCAENOG FOREST, EAST

The silence of the spruces is absolute, the tiny road deserted, the land uneven, untidy as the sky. Large, grey-floored clearings in the forest disclose distant blue mountain ranges, and small Welsh trees flourish by a wandering stream. Old walls are vividly patterned with lichens, black and white over the grey. The forest is not quite continuous – it is broken in places by green farms full of fat sheep. The silence is broken too, sometimes, by a noise of diesels, for the landscape, despite its purity, is that of a highly mechanized timber-production industry, spread over 10,000 acres. It is spread out in time too, for the trees impose a very slow rhythm, and there are miles of twilight here where nothing perceptible happens for twenty years at a time. The forest floor is deep, piled with millions of leaves measuring two centimetres by two millimetres, each marked with ten lines of tiny dots – stomata – perfectly geometrical but, like finger prints, never matching any other. These are the leaves of Sitka spruces and the trees were planted here, of course, but they grow as their ancestors must have grown two million years ago above these ancient rocks, gregarious and containing darkness. There are quantities of the squashy, cylindrical cones, each one bearing who knows how many useless seeds, and grey, dead twigs, rather bony-looking. Many shining, clean

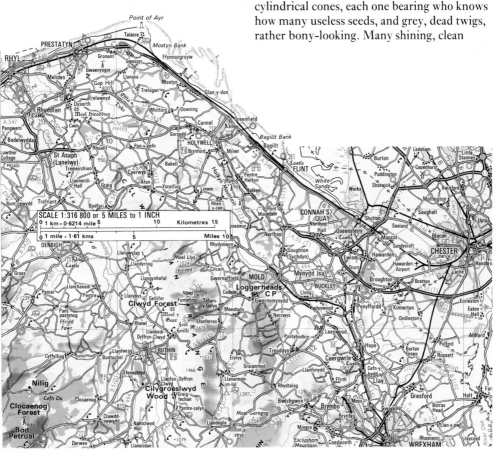

Amanita muscaria, Clocaenog Forest

fungi nose their way from the dampness below, among them the fiery red, white-spotted, globes of the hallucinogenic fly agaric, *Amanita muscaria* – strange fruit for grey, chapel-going North Wales.

A web of thin, irregular roads meets on the forest plateau at a signpost marked (north-east) Cyffylliog, (south) Llanfihangel, (north) Denbigh – and indeed you can go all the way to Denbigh on the same narrow roads, 8 miles in all. South-west is to Pentre-llyn-cymmer near the Alwen Reservoir. Forestry roads of gravel weave a complex pattern amongst these remote highways, and all are open to the walker, or even the driver, daring the Commission's wrath.

Nilig *017 549*, ♀ ♠ , *picnic place, FC*
On the road from Cyffylliog, mentioned above, this picnic place is hardly necessary for there

Clocaenog Forest

are dozens of places to stop further into the forest. But it is a pretty spot, with a group of young lodgepole pines, and a stream with sallows and rowans, by a lichenous stone bridge. The Forestry Commission has planted some of its stock amenity trees: Norway maples and one or two white poplars, as if to deny the beauty of the conifers. Heather and gorse are pretty too.

Bod Petrual *037 511*, ♀ ♠, *2 walks, FC*
Bod Petrual is a Visitors' Centre in a whitewashed cottage, by a charming lake half full of water-horsetail and surrounded by oaks, ashes, larches, pines and Norway spruces. Nothing stirred in early October except an old Welshman with two bulging plastic bags – could they be full of fly agaric? Some Sitka spruces are thickly planted round about and fairly mature; the cones were so large and the foliage so rich that I had to check they were Sitka. Lichens are richly represented here as well as fungi. Walks range from a waymarked

$\frac{1}{4}$ mile, surely not too taxing, to $2\frac{3}{4}$ miles. The cottage wouldn't open for me, but it contains an interpretive display. The leaflet reproduces part of the former owner Lord Bagot's planting plan, and gives the Welsh names of the trees.

A viewpoint car park is 1 mile north-east, the view being over the nice country of the

Bridge at Nilig

From the viewpoint car park at the eastern side of Clocaenog Forest, *053 520*

Helleborus foetidus, Cilygroeslwyd, October

Clwyd Valley. Beyond is the Llantysilio Mountain and others.

NEAR RUTHIN

Cilygroeslwyd Wood *126 553, ♀, 10 acres, NR*

This is a patch of ashwood with the odd yew and some hazel on Carboniferous limestone, not much of a walk but a valuable nature reserve. Take the Corwen or Bala road, the A494(T), south from Ruthin, and turn left at the sign 'Llanfair DC'. There is parking space over the little bridge (and a good view of the hills). The wood lies 250 yards beyond a wooden stile in the iron fence along the main road.

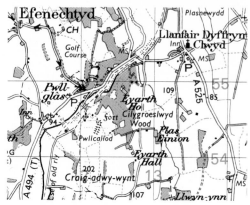

Clwyd Forest *173 612, (♀)♠, 1500 acres, trails, fairly steep, FC*

East of Ruthin the beautiful sequence of hills running north and south has a focus for walkers at Moel Famau, 1772 feet. You can walk all the way on Forestry Commission land, 3½ miles, all uphill. There is a forestry trail leaflet, if you can get it. The narrow road to the parking place is signed from the A494(T) at the Llanferres end. It is a sort of short cut to Ruthin which ends in a hairpin at Llanbedr DC (where it is not signposted). Coming from Ruthin, take the second or third turning left after the petrol station in Llanbedr. The car park is shaped like a railway siding, and has electric cables running over it. It serves the Country Park of Moel Famau (2375 acres of heath and mountain top). It boasts a grandiose lavatory block with perspex domes where I

Erratic boulder and attenuated rowan, Moel Famau

spent an agonized hour persuading a blue tit to fly out of the door.

Trees planted by the road are larches, chestnut and, a bit surprising, laburnum. It should be pointed out that laburnum seeds can be fatal in quite small quantities, and while no doubt the effect of the granite loos surrounded by brilliant yellow blossom in early summer is impressive, the whole adds up to an ecological nonsense, with hazards for birds and children. But straight forest roads and dark bands of forest trees subtly emphasize the curves of this glacial valley, and the foresters have left even straighter rowans, which grew up amongst the larches. I examined a boulder, an erratic of some sort of conglomerate, which the glacier had left at the bottom of its lake. In the intervening 10,000 years some moss had grown on its reticulated surface and, shaped like a miniature of the hills around it, it caused me to reflect that even Forestry Commissions come and go, and the apparently indestructible plastic bags stuck in the gorse, the granite loo, the electricity cables and the gregarious multicoloured cars – and you and I – are all very temporary.

Loggerheads, *198 627*, a mile east, is a Country Park and a Site of Special Scientific Interest, on limestone, which outcrops in impressive cliffs on the next line of hills.

Index